The Bible & I

The Bible & I

E. M. Blaiklock

BETHANY HOUSE PUBLISHERS
MINNEAPOLIS, MINNESOTA 55438
A Division of Bethany Fellowship, Inc.

Originally published in Great Britain by Marshall
Morgan & Scott

ISBN 0-87123-298-7

Published by Bethany House Publishers
A Division of Bethany Fellowship, Inc.
6820 Auto Club Road, Minneapolis, MN 55438

Printed in the United States of America

Contents

1: I and three Books

We have been together a long time, the Bible and I, almost a lifetime, and companionship has not lost its freshness and its inspiration. It is barely a mile away in a straight line below the window of the library where I sit, to the place where the little cottage stood at the shaggy southwestern edge of the city I have seen grow. It is all suburban real-estate down there, but lost amid the houses and the gardens is the ghost of the landscape I knew when I was a small boy. That was where my sanguine father thought to farm the hungry clay, fresh though he was from the skills of Tangye's steam engineering works in sombre old Birmingham.

That was a brave venture which brought him little joy and no material reward. But in the house he built with his own hands on those unrewarding acres, he had a wealth of culture stored in many books. Richly he passed it on to me. A lonely little boy I absorbed it all, and in years and years of exploration in the bush-filled uplands and the infinitely varied shores of the mighty and empty Manukau, I made literature mine. How full of health and wealth can loneliness be. I made a Narnia in which I loved and grew.

It was then, it was there, that I first read the Bible, a sturdy book whose cover had been bent and creased in a cabin trunk on our long journey out through Suez and Australia. I had a small bunk-room at the veranda's end with a desk built in beside the cosy bed. There was a shelf of books above, but the Bible lay at hand on the desk-top by the heavy glass inkwell, and I often read a little from it in a pool of soft light from the kerosene lamp. I had references in the margins and I learned, in curiosity, how to use them, and at times puzzled over how these words referred to those.

It is odd how the wraith of those pages survives. I suppose I have over two hundred copies of the whole or portions of Scripture round me in this long book-filled room on the edge of what is still the bush, mercifully rejuvenating after the loot and ravage of the pioneers who came to this land not too long before we came ourselves. I have Bibles old and new in eight languages. Some of them are exquisite samples of the printer's and the binder's art. And yet there are one or two passages which, in the mind's eye, I still envisage in the columned pages of my first Bible, there beside my bed.

I remember well reading often in the Passion story, trying to fit into one the four accounts, and experiencing a strange sensation of suspended history. I knew the end. I knew that they crucified him, but the tension held me through the trial. Surely it could not be that these scoundrels would have their way! I even sensed vaguely that there was something unsaid, something behind the scenes in John's account. Could a Roman be so oddly dominated by those he was there to govern and control? I read back in Matthew and thought about that bowl of water. I was a third-former at the Grammar School and we read Macbeth that year. It shot into my mind when we read of the woman's guilty hand which would rather 'the multitudinous seas incarnadine . . .' that here was Pilate too.

It must have been a little later in my secondary school years that I began to read almost exclusively in the Fourth Gospel. 'Ye must be born again . . .' How it baffled me. And yet, I thought, turning in my mind the other words which always haunted me, could I do better or other than what I was doing, listening to the words of Christ, by reading John who knew him? The 'other words' came from the headmaster's prayer read in school assembly in the high majestic hall every morning: 'And while we grow in earthly knowledge may we also grow in the knowledge of our Lord and Saviour Jesus Christ . . .'

I am surprised, looking back on those and earlier days, that I found the Levitical Law fascinating. On the edge of the wilderness where bolder Aucklanders were beginning to settle on the cheap land, and brave the clattering railway into town, there was little Christian witness. As a very small boy I attended a small brick Congregational church, which still stands among a welter of shops and industry. An old lady, wife of a retired Presbyterian minister, taught one group of which I was a fascinated member. She told us all about the meaning of the Hebrew sacrificial law, what the altar and the offerings meant, and the meaning of what Moses taught his rescued tribes to do in that awesome wilderness. It might be imagined that such pabulum was hardly fit for ten-year olds, but it held me with deepest interest, and it was there that I first made acquaintance with the Old Testament.

But not all Leviticus and Numbers. A dynamic young man appeared at the beginning of one year and assembled our group in a wooden shed attached to the church. Sitting tilted back on his chair, he told us the story of Joseph, with such magnificent colour and realism that I looked forward with sharp anticipation to the coming Sunday. He did it again, finished the story of Joseph and promised us that of Moses. He announced the prize of a book for the best written account of what he had been telling us of the shepherd lad who had become a vizier in Egypt. I knew that word because I was deep in the Arabian Nights at home.

In my first major venture into writing, I spent the week writing the story of Joseph, and modernising the words of my bedside Bible. I took the pages to the church on the following Sunday, but the dynamic wizard with words was not there, and never came again.

I think my Bible with the damaged cover went away in the year following the second war, when some organisation made a great effort to collect and export to ravaged lands, and even to a burnt, blitzed Britain, any texts of Scripture which could be of use. I hope the book, which went for many years with me, achieved a second career, and taught other eyes to see.

Only two other Bibles have widely accompanied me. Soon after I became a Christian as a University freshman, I bought a cloth-bound Bible with Dr. Scofield's references, and it accompanied me abroad to Europe in 1924 when, between my reading for a bachelor's degree and for a master's, I had what the Germans call a 'wanderyear'. Dr. Scofield taught me some theology, but I was not slow to see that his eschatology did not match what Scripture actually had to say. Three year's intensive study in the methods and criteria of literary and historical criticism had made me aware of the need for rigorous testing of evidence. I took the volume with me because it was neatly paragraphed and plainly printed. I had it bound in black morocco leather by a craftsman in the trade in Leyton where I lodged. The poor man charged me five shillings and the book lies beside me on my desk this late spring evening, its leather hardly showing the wear of half a century. It lays open in my hand flat and wide like the Bible Billy Graham always seems to use.

The other book is my late lamented Greek Testament. I had it bound likewise in black leather with my name upon it, and last year left it in a hotel by Galilee, perhaps a good place to lose it, if it is better to lose such a small treasure in any one place more than in another. That little book, slim in its India-paper, travelled almost a million miles with me, six hundred thousand in the air alone. It accompanied me to some twenty-five countries. It lay in a dozen famous pulpits for, at least when I read the Gospels to a congregation, I commonly read a new translation directly from the Greek text. It is not as convenient so to read Paul, because his sentences (the opening of Ephesians, for example) can be convoluted, and it is difficult in a quick translation to hold two ends of a long sentence simultaneously in the compass of the eye.

I have read from that little book at the Keswick Convention and in All Souls, Langham Place, in Fifth Avenue and Hollywood Presbyterian, in Calvary Baptist Church, in

Australian and New Zealand cathedrals, and how many other places. In the task of taking groups of pilgrims to the sites of the Bible, I have read from it at the Garden Tomb the story of the race of Peter and John to the holy place, and the Beatitudes from the magnolia covered slope above the silver level of Galilee where they were spoken. In the synagogues of Capernaum and of Nazareth, up the grim little Arab suq, I have read and translated the right words from that precious little book. On the bema at Corinth, I have read aloud in their crackling Greek the words with which Gallio dismissed the insensitive Jews, too foolish to keep 'a low profile' after Claudius had expelled them from Rome.

On the Areopagus under the magnificent shadow of the Parthenon, I have read in Luke's Greek Paul's clever speech and translated it. I have paraphrased the town-clerk's oration in the theatre of Ephesus and shown how one letter, in one word – 'proconsuls' – authenticates it. I have used the same little volume on the site of all the seven churches of Revelation except Thyatira, where it is difficult in the small market town to find a holy site. I have stood on the Roman paving in the road west which runs through the village of Emmaus, and read the tale of the two walking home, dull-eyed, when a Stranger joined them on the way and stayed to supper. Driving into Corinth I have read the thirteenth chapter of the first letter to that disordered little church, and watched the driver and the guide striving to catch the meaning when I read the ancient words in Greek, which modern Greek tongues have so distorted. I have read Jude's benediction in the Athens Evangelical Church by the Arch of Hadrian, and told of Peter where the long curve of the beach at Joppa sweeps north into the smog of Tel Aviv along its curve of sandy shore.

Yes, I and that little book have travelled much together. The time passes, but I still retain the hope that someone will find the neat volume, read my name and post it back across the world to me. I have another that fits my pocket, but its leather does not lay open so demurely in my hand,

and there are no personal memories, along with eternal truth, lying between its covers.

Three Bibles and I – one gone to Europe, one lost at Tiberias, and one here beside me. It still serves, because among my smaller journalistic tasks is the provision each day of a text for our largest newspaper. I tick off in the margin each one I use.

But, you will not need to be told, the Bible is greater than any bound pages which hold its message in printers' ink. The Bible can live in the tissues of the mind. How much of it went in rolls of vellum or papyrus across the desert to exile in Babylon? And yet, if my pondering over the Psalms is correct, it was 'by the rivers of Babylon' that the Old Testament was put together, as far as it was known, to be a stay and a standard for those who had nothing more now than their Book round which a broken nation could at all cohere. It was in their hearts and mind that it lived. It could, perhaps, be done again. I could myself reconstruct the whole Greek text of John, and a good deal more.

But I have other thoughts to put on paper. These words are only preface to what I can more usefully say. I shall try to tell what the Bible had meant to me, how I learned, as a classicist, intelligently to read it, of the impact of certain parts of it upon heart and mind . . . I shall tell of personalities which have come to mean much to me, of the tools and methods of studying and understanding . . . The Bible and I . . . Yes we have together travelled far, and how much further there remains to go I do not know, but we cannot be separated now. I shall riffle the pages and perhaps let out some truth that will pass through my fingers – like Don Richardson in the West Irian hut finding a way to release the message of John 3:16. The men looked amazed, as he sprang the message for them out of the little cluster of leaves in his hand that held the story of 'the Peace Child' trapped within. I shall try then to tell what the Bible has meant to me and how the understanding came. It will be the record of an adventure, long as life, of the mind and spirit, of the discovery of the Word within the Word, of a literature born of man, but breathed of God.

The Bible is more than any Bible. It is more than words printed, written on papyrus, parchment, vellum, paper. 'Biblia' they called it, and the word is plural, for the Bible is composed of books which cover two millennia of man. The Bible has demanded much of me, in study, thought, patience and striving to understand. It has challenged faith, probed my personality. It has called for rigorous academic scrutiny and demanded reading far beyond the limits of its text. It has been a lamp to my feet and a light to my path. I shall need it still to illumine the path as the shadows begin to lengthen over 'the little landscape of my life'. Here then is the story of a personal encounter with what my hands have handled of the word of life.

2: The Bible in the Twenties

The twenties of this century, that curious, tense aftermath of the first war's ravage, were for me, by God's good grace, a time of intense and formative intellectual activity. Those years saw uncommonly decisive events, five years of student life, bisected by that stimulating 'wanderyear', some arduous teaching as a language master, my marriage, life's greatest fortune, and the first three demanding years in the Classics Department where I was to remain until 1968.

Above all, amid events so final in their life's significance, I became a Christian, in May, 1921, the climax, as such decision is for those whose head rules, of much pondering. And that story I have told elsewhere.

It was the beginning of long thought about the Bible, an activity interwoven with all the deep study and wide reading that my responsibilities in teaching ancient languages and literature imposed on me. And how fortunate I was to be thrust into a career so relevant, to know daily the rigour and exactions of the skills and scholarship that finest and oldest of disciplines demands. It steadied me, equipped me, and led me to the conclusions I shall attempt to share.

I knew without a doubt that a solid Christian faith could only stand if it was held and buttressed by a Bible which could feed the heart and satisfy the mind, a Word as living as the Lord which it presented. And through the Church was running that wind of liberalism largely fanned by the hapless people whom we had just fought down all along that red swathe which the First World War had made through the history of man. I had little time to read the sorry books which were seeking to recondition the Scriptures and reanimate a newly made Christ into some sort of young Apollo or greater Galahad, but I could well see how small a future there was for a Christianity based on what in those days we called 'modernism'.

I knew that historic truth was as vital for a faith based on the Bible, as it was in the correct interpretation of the Latin and Greek writers it was my daily duty to teach and to expound. I knew something of the great Biblical scholars of the decades immediately before. James Orr, and James Denney, those great Presbyterians, mightily helped me. Denney's insistence that a theology must be something which can be salutarily and convincingly preached, heightened my interest in the sturdy evangelist, Reuben Arthur Torrey, whose active career lasted until 1928. I came to Christ through the preached word and early began to propagate it in the pulpit, as a reasonable, a Biblical, and I hoped a convincing message. I also discovered before that decade's end, the work of William Mitchell Ramsay, who held me for many years as a classicial historian and archaeologist.

But I was conscious of a great gap in a conservative scholarship. I was equally aware that with the enormous field of classical literature open and awaiting my thought and reading as a professional classicist, I was not yet in a position to investigate as widely as I should have wished the literary and historical problems of the Bible. I found the evangelical and conservative Christians into whose warm company my commitment to Christ had brought me, and who were, I was keenly aware, correct basically in their zeal for a traditional and a conservative view of the Bible, held as orthodox a nexus of opinions, forms of exegesis, and prescriptions which in no way stood the tests I was in the habit of applying to the documents of the past which were my daily area of investigation.

Dr. C. I. Scofield, whose annotated Scriptures I acquired, as I described in my words of introduction, were quite generally accepted in orthodox circles as expressing a prescribed view for preaching and teaching. Scofield, had I known it, had no great qualifications for the role so widely and generously accorded him. It was simply that he had no rivals of trusted standing and authority. He was born in 1843, served with distinction under Lee in the awful American Civil War, qualified for the legal profession in 1869, and produced his Bible in 1909, forty years later. In other words, in education, reading and professional study, he had much less by way of relevent qualifications to pronounce on the meaning of Scripture than I had in my own early career, and far less still in later years. Scofield died in 1921.

His survey of doctrine was austere, strong and traditional, and I use that word in its best sense. Where he did much damage was in his treatment of prophecy, the true meaning of which he disguised, his eschatological planning, and his bizarre treatment of apocalyptic literature. It became an article of faith to accept, for example, those immensely interesting chapters in the Book of the Revelation, which contain the letters 'to the seven churches', as a preview of history. Such views were astonishingly tenacious. I remember, as late as 1959, finding my own 'soundness' doubted in a San Francisco gathering when I sought to show what Relevation 2 and 3 were really about.

It is also the way of man to exceed a mandate, and Dr Scofield was outdistanced by his disciples. I remember hearing a sermon by a notable expert in 'prophecy' from Sydney, on the sad and illuminating little book of Haggai, in which the message was related to a diabolical role which Turkey was to play in eschatological events in the twenties. Another group, whose teaching activities continue to the phenomenon of the EEC, was watching excitedly for the emergence of the Roman Empire. I remember how crestfallen was the worthy old soldier who was a caretaker in my wing of the University when Erwin Rommel could not, in the end, make it to the Nile. Egypt, as the Emperor Augustus would have agreed, was the most vital province in the Mediterranean and a most essential part of the Roman Empire. It had to fall to Germany.

In two other spheres of doctrine, largely supported and popularised by the Scofield Bible, the master was outbidden by his disciples. 'Typology' is an example, that notion that events, persons, objects in history can, under divine ordinance, prefigure events, persons, objects yet to be. Scripture gives a certain justification for this view, adapted to the eastern rather than to the western mind. It can scarcely be denied, as the old teacher in the little Congregational church patiently informed my childhood, that the Levitical law had an educative function. The complicated system taught a debased and brutalised people fresh from an Egyptian 'archipelago' of labour camps, the oneness and supremacy of God in every detail of life, it linked death and sin, its system of dedication and offering bypassed and checked some loathsome practices of contemporary paganism. Archaeology increasingly shows how lucid and how special in Moses' hands the symbolism of the ceremonial law was.

The beautiful desert tent, the Tabernacle, its prescriptions so significantly given right after the sorry lapse of the tribes under Sinai, when they tried to set God forth in the semblance of the Egyptian bull-god Apis, was also a remarkable symbol. It taught by its lovely presence that God was among them, beaten by the same wilderness sandstorms, under the same heat and chill, but unseen, to be only approached by reverence and due forms of worship. It does indeed carry a glimmer of what was to be when one 'tabernacled among us.'

Hebrews and Galatians especially use events and details from the Old Testament as types (if we are prepared to build whole systems of exegesis on such words as those of Romans 5:14, with Adam a 'type of one who was to come'), but it must be remembered that the Hebrew mind was conditioned and bent to think in the framework and the forms of the Old Testament. That is why the symbol of the good Melchisedek, the mysterious king of Jerusalem, was a far more powerful symbol of truth to an educated Hebrew than it would be to a Greek; notable and clear to anyone familiar with Greek thought is the Hellenism of the learned writer of the epistle to the Galatians.

But grant the truth of all this, and the nonsense of much of that which passed for accepted orthodoxy in the preaching and teaching of the twenties still remains. It was damaging to some educated people who were not steadied by the thought that documents of vital importance cannot be thrown out by the folly of one absurd or manifestly wrong interpretation. By chance I came simultaneously on an illustration from the Greek epic. I had read with incredulity the only foolish book that the great classical scholar, Gilbert Murray, ever wrote. Taking the documentary theory of the Pentateuch with undue seriousness (it is often unwise for a scholar to treat with uncritical acceptance, 'assured results' from another discipline) Murray wrote of the patchwork emergence of Homer's two great epics, the Iliad and the Odyssey. The result was complete absurdity, and fortunately (always a salutary idea) I had read the two epics carefully before discovering Murray's *Rise of the Greek Epic*, which he wrote in 1904. It still forms a striking illustration of the odd light which disciplined application of the norms of classical literary and historical criticism can throw on some of the once popular extravagances of Biblical criticism.

Fortunately, in time to bolster my instinctive reaction, J. A. Scott's *Unity of Homer* came out in 1921, and I will say no more of this small experience. The point I am seeking to make is that a novel and plausible view, or some bold departure from the traditional, is not by any means likely to be the final word. But in Biblical teaching, I did see young Christians thrown off balance by dogmatically advocated views of orthodoxy, which, on the grounds of their academic training in varied spheres of study, they saw to be unscholarly and out of tune with their ways of thought.

I can remember with some vividness three encounters with the typology which raised these questions, and one with the so-called 'dispensationalism' which also marked (and marred) the 'Scofield' approach to Scripture. I found a small book on the Tabernacle which proceeded to claim deep spiritual and theological truth in the colours of the material, the length and decoration of the cordage, the minute detail of the specification and all else to the point where intelligence rebelled. The whole exercise in the desert was a lesson in detailed obedience. On that I could agree.

There is no greater unifying force in history, as Toynbee (whom I was to find an important influence on my thinking) noted, than a common task to perform in demanding detail for a concerted end. But here was 'obscurantism', to an unacceptable degree. I did not in such rejection, cast aside the meaning of the altar, the sacred box, the mercy seat, the holy of holies (a symbol, the discovery of Hazor has shown, known more widely among Semitic tribes, than Moses' moving adaptation).

My second illustration was from an eloquent address by a man of fine but utterly undisciplined intelligence, on the fate of the worthless Haman (hardly a worse character, be it confessed, than his designing Jewish foe, Mordecai). Haman and his ten sons, ironically hoisted on the gallows built for another victim, signified the Antichrist and the Ten Kings.

Those dynasts of the revived Roman Empire, would not leave the halls of conservative evangelicals during those vital and formative years in which I shaped my own views of the Bible. The ten fragile toes of Daniel's image to be smashed by the descending rock of Christ, were, of course, standard belief. It was useless to point out that the two legs could hardly sustain the imagery of the Western and Eastern Roman Empire, when, in historical certainty, Rome in the West crumbled under the impact of the Gothic invasions in the fifth century, whereas, in the East, Byzantium, or Constantinople, endured until the hideous inroad of the Moslem Turks into Asia Minor and Europe, with the decisive moment in 1453 when the great city fell.

'Even now,' said John, 'there are many Antichrists', but in the twenties the quest was on. How true that word has been in this twentieth century which, as Herbert Butterfield said in 1948, has more points of similarity with the century in which the New Testament was born than has any one of the rest which lie between.

But the search for the Man of Sin in the twenties was a preoccupation of those bemused by prophecy such as we have not seen since. The German Kaiser having been satisfactorily relegated to lumbering on a Dutch estate, eyes were alert elsewhere. Sun Yat Sen merited a glance. So did Kemal Ataturk, whom we at this world's end had abundant reason to dislike. I have stood in his ruined bunker just below Sari Bair, for the man led his troops from the front, unlike Sir Ian Hamilton, safely cabined out of range. The Anzacs had no chance fighting uphill against his riflemen, but Kemal hardly qualified as Antichrist . . . 'Watch Mussolini', whispered another sage I heard.

I am not denying that the Monster lurks in the background of what Paul hinted and John. It is a sombre fact that in a computer-ridden, shrunken world, Revelation's thirteenth chapter could be horribly fulfilled. Nor would I, nor did I, question for a moment that Christ spoke in clear terms of an end-time, and a second intrusion into human history, but it was as obvious that he also veiled the time in mystery. It was tragic to see Christians, whose food of mind and heart is the Scriptures, starved with such material as that which so many pulpits within my early area of Christian activity dispensed. It was more tragic to see young people disappointed in the Bible and abandoning Christianity because what they were taught about the Bible, proved so rapidly disappointing and untrue. Those who thought more deeply and perhaps read more widely, were unshaken, as I was. By the mercy of Heaven, I saw the culpable weakness of some 'fundamentalist' attitudes, and kept my independence of mind without lurching towards the 'modernist' school which so arrogantly professed to speak for my mind.

The other encounter (I mentioned three) which stays in my mind was a small book on the Song of Solomon by, I think, the veteran missionary, Hudson Taylor. No one with any training in the reading of ancient literature would think of taking that small piece of Hebrew lyric poetry for other than it is, a love song, perhaps an epithalamium or wedding piece, difficult to analyse because we lack some dramatic, choric, or even musical ground-plan. Taylor sought to popularise a spiritualised allegorical interpretation as old, I know now, as rabbinical literature, and adopted, since the days of the early Christians by many who could not bear to see the love of man and woman dealt with in a sacred Scripture – for all the acceptance of the wedding-feast of Cana in the narrative of the New Testament. I had to confess that I found the attempt to identify the Shulamite with the Bride of Christ, and to force the lush imagery of the song into a statement of union between the Church and its Lord, something close to revolting. Again I was largely left to my own thinking in the evangelical circles in which I walked and had rightly chosen to walk. Young Christians today do not realise how fortunate they are with the wealth they have at their disposal of scholarly conservative litera-ture on the Bible, which can inform and shape their minds, and in no way offend the principles of scholarship they accept in other spheres of their academic life.

Another concept I found difficult to accommodate as a student of history and literature was 'dispensationalism.' The word occurs four times in the New Testament. It is 'oikonomia' from which we derive the word 'economy.' Paul uses it twice for the conduct of the apostolate, once for the administration of a household, and twice for God's plan of salvation. Obviously there is offered no theological or historical justification here for a stratification of God's dealing with man into periods in which the requirements of salvation are variously and differently defined, seven clearly marked eras, according to Scofield, my main au-thority, following S. N. Darby, who himself gathered threads going back to Augustine. As far as I could see, directly approaching the documents, the golden thread of faith tied it all together, and made a unity for the timeless in historic time from Abraham to Paul and Hebrews. I think I passed a climax of rejection when I heard a lecture from an exegete of the order, explaining that the Lord's Prayer should not be used because it belonged to 'the King-dom Age', for, he challenged us, 'would we care to be forgiven only as we forgive'? Whether such nonsense and denial of the plain direction of Christ actually denied any of the audience the comfort and blessing of that blessed rosary of words, I do not know, but it decided me that 'dispensationalism' had its perils, and chief among them was that it could make the intelligent impatient.

'Premillennialism' and the question of the Church and 'the great tribulation', was another live subject of theological and exegetical debate, wasteful in the extreme of time, energy and unity, within the faith. So was Darwinism. When I became a foundation member of the Inter-Varsity-Fellowship in Auckland, I discovered to my distress that the textbook for their studies was on 'Creation or Evolution.' Whose was the greater folly in that confrontation between science and religion, dating from the foolish debate between Huxley and Wilberforce, is difficult to determine. Was it the Darwinists who maintained that a speculative theory of how things came about, banished from the whole teleological process the Mind behind phenomena which seemed to be as much as ever demanded, or the zealous defenders of the faith who were frightened or daunted by the absurd assumption? I did not know, and had early learned that in academic circles one should not too rashly invade an unfamiliar discipline. I had already heard too many preachers and amateur theologians quoting Greek. When, in 1927, I became a lecturer in the University, I was able to take a firmer hand in matters of student Christian witness, and divert the energies of their study into more certain and more profitable areas.

I was conscious of how, during my first ten years as a Christian, I sought for an identity and an intellectual climate in which to breathe and find congenial fellowship, and I was steadied in two ways. I discovered such men as those I have mentioned, Orr and Denney. I also discovered Paul of Tarsus, first through Dean Farrar's great book, discovered in a second-hand shop, and through Conybeare and Howson's similar biography. Both books set a course for me as a classicist of which I shall say more. I realised what vast areas of certainty there were wide-open to explore, and how futile it was to waste time in uncertainties, speculation and trivialities.

The other steadying force was in my own academic training. I knew that the first task in understanding a document, any piece of literature or history, was to ask what it has to say, to read it, in a word. Only then is it profitable, and, for a teacher or student, necessary to turn to what others have to say about it. For example, turning to those early chapters of Genesis, all that the Bible seemed to me to say was that the dictate of God lay behind created things. It seemed also to say that he proceeded in an ordered sequence and that his first edict was a deep mystery. He called light into being, a word the writer of Hebrews has in mind when he says that the measurable universe of physical science emerged from that which eludes all measurement, the seen from the unseen. As far as my mind can comprehend about the preoccupations of subatomic physics today, the Bible, two millennia and four millennia ago, seems to have said in simple speech all that can be said today. Whatever it is that we call matter would seem to have receded from comprehension like an exploding galaxy.

Looking further I found man described as made from the raw material of nature, fragile molecules mysteriously bonded, but built into a thing of wonder by the inbreathing of God. He was given liberty, only to be real if tested by a prohibition. And so it came about that man used freedom ill and produced the world we know. I could not answer then, as I cannot answer now, what moved God to do or to allow, but I see no point in waiting for such an answer. There is the obvious fact that man has sinned and marred his world, that God is so intimately involved in that situation that he undertook extraordinary measures to produce a 'way of salvation', and had I not myself begun my Christian pilgrimage at the beginning of the decade as an experiment, a 'doing of his will' on Christ's own guarantee that thus I should 'know the doctrine'?

Amid the confusion of those years, I should have liked to find a rallying-point. The Bible and I came through together, not by a refusal to open my mind, but by a conviction that the right direction must finally reach the right goal. There was no other road in the direction I sensed was right. Modernism, oddly enough at first a Roman Catholic invention, finally scotched during his pontificate

(1903–1914) by Pius X as a 'synthesis of all heresies', could only be an arid and a moribund radicalism by which many were finding their way out of the Church and into agnosticism. There were those briefly to the front who described themselves as 'liberal Protestants' who professed as the *Oxford Dictionary of the Christian Church* puts it 'an anti-dogmatic and humanitarian reconstruction of the Christian faith.' The Student Christian Movement was sickening of that odd malady. The term 'liberal evangelical'. which was also current, was one step nearer to basic essentials. Its exponents claimed 'to restate old truths', said the same authority, for example the atonement and the authority of the Bible, in terms more consonant with modern thought. With that aim I agreed. I have always endeavoured to bear it in mind in all I have said and written about the Bible, but there is an overriding requirement: the content must not be leached out in the process, and as Denney required, a preachable Gospel must emerge. I did not find either Barth or Brunner, who appeared in my sky, provided what I needed. The word 'liberal' haunted all such reconstruction. It is a pity that, in so many spheres of human thought and activity, that word and its cognates have arrogantly assumed meanings which are far from what a pure concept of liberty should mean.

And it was a pity about 'fundamentalism.' The word contained all and much more of those oddities of interpretation and exegesis than I could accept. The separatism, polemical and passionately controversial approach which so often accompanied such profession, also alienated me, though I had no sympathy with the term 'obscurantism', levelled against the fundamentalist by the more arrogant of equally intolerant liberals. The word suggests willfull opposition to the light, and goes back to a German sixteenth century satire against scholasticism.

What a test of patience and tolerance (and I believe intolerance) it all was. How hard it was for a professional teacher of ancient languages and literature to listen, for example to denunciations of the 'higher critics', who not without reason as I shall try to show in the next chapter, were equated with those dedicated to dissecting the Bible complacently to death. Need I define my terms?

Higher criticism, in spite of that common misuse of the term, is a neutral and technical term. The 'lower criticism' is the objective examination of a text in order to establish the correct reading. It involves paleography, the collation, history, and descent of manuscripts. The lower critic is concerned with meaning only in so far as his goal is to determine what the writer clearly said. His task is largely mechanical and the more impersonal the better. The 'higher critic' takes over where he leaves off.

For example, in John 5:4, it is impossible to establish on 'lower critical' grounds whether or not the verse should have a place in the text. Did John write those words or did he not? The manuscripts are evenly divided. The case is therefore referred to the higher critical court, where meaning, relevance, the harmony of the verse with the theme of the book or the teaching of the Bible, context, historical, literary, religious, and such wider themes are brought into consideration. The case, in such a discussion, is overwhelmingly against the authenticity of the verse we have used for illustration, for no other competitive miracle had a place in the Bible, and the Lord, in his cure, disregarded the pool. It is a 'gloss,' a marginal explanation which has intruded into the text.

John 8:1–11 provides a similar illustration. The lower critical evidence is likewise inconclusive. But in the higher critical court the passage is overwhelmingly vindicated. It is so true to life, so consonant with Christ's teaching and manners, that its authenticity cannot be doubted. John may have included a note written by a colleague in his text. Hence some odd words. Early monasticism accounts for its wide deletion. And let it not be thought that the New Testament is ridden with such dilemmas. There are only one or two, and much less significant passages, of similar difficulty.

Such is 'higher criticism.' How came it then that the term is still popularly used for modernism? The fault is with those who abused the critical process, infused judgment with prejudice, and used a delicate branch of scholarship to hawk private opinion. Let us use the term technically. Beside this, conservative criticism is now on its feet and is indeed dominant.

3: Informed Conservatism

With the clarity of hindsight, and with the widening view as life's road climbs, it is possible to see how the storm and stress of those years befell the Church, and made the way so difficult for a young Christian scholar, who prized integrity, to walk steadily in the way.

I was intensely involved in my work. The teaching load in the University was a heavy one, but there is no place where the mind finds more challenge, where honest zeal for truth and objective interpretation is more severely tested than in a University Classics School. And I should add there are no studies more relevant to the Bible and its understanding than those which have intimately to do with those languages and literatures, and those centuries of history in which the Bible was born and grew.

We were a widely based Department. Until the death of A. C. Paterson, my beloved chief, Semitics were part of our curriculum, and although the teaching of Hebrew was never unloaded on to me, other centuries than those behind Latin and Greek were part of our consciousness, and had their place in our library.

Intense study and heavy work were the mark of my twenties. In my thirties, after Paterson's death, and when a less demanding Department emerged, I had years of abundant opportunity to read and develop those spheres of expertise which have since been my preoccupation. Seven years devoted only to teaching Greek preceded my appointment to the Chair of Classics. An extraordinary training.

But I was a convinced conservative at the age of thirty. I should perhaps add a hopeful adjective to the word 'conservative.' I last talked with that old stalwart, Dr. Graham Scroggie, in 1951, at his home in Wimbledon. We discussed the present theme. He held up a large hand with fingers spread. He clasped the uplifted thumb with his other hand and said: 'Modernist'; then likewise the little finger, saying: 'Obscurantist.' He gripped the forefinger with the word: 'Liberal,' and the third finger saying: 'Fundamentalist.' The tall middle finger remained, straight and challenging. He seized it and wagged it. 'Informed Conservative,' he said, 'there I stand.' Obviously, Dr Scroggie was protesting against the partisanship sometimes mistaken for orthodoxy. He was not in any way pleading for compromise or a perilous progress down the middle of the road. All who knew him know that he yielded to none in his respect for the authority and inspiration of Scripture. He did, however, demand that orthodoxy should not be a mere emotional attitude, but the stand of an informed, devoted man, and free from both credulity and superstition, and the noise and controversy which has so often passed for scholarship. When, therefore, I claim to be 'a convinced conservative,' I hope also to be regarded as 'an informed conservative.'

It is well to state with the greatest possible clarity what it is that the informed conservative is trying to preserve. Here lies much misunderstanding, occasioned, no doubt, by extravagant statements on both sides.

The principal object of his jealous conservation is an authoritative Bible. He cannot see how, without the loftiest doctrine of inspiration, that which Scripture teaches can be advanced, preached, or taught with cogency or confidence. Granted a Bible sanctioned by God, he can preach without misgiving the traditional message of Christianity – a divine Christ, an atoning death, a unified Bible with a nation's history moulded to the end of God's inruption into history, and a unified New Testament with no dichotomy between Christ and Paul. Once shake substantially the authority of Scripture, and the haphazard collection of documents into which the Bible forthwith dissolves, becomes a happy hunting ground for theorists. Interpretation, devout or clever, becomes rationalist, subjective, secular. The Bible ceases to speak, if it is no longer the Word of God. Nor does it solve the dilemma to state that, amid a welter of human gropings, it merely contains the Word of God. Authority must be objective, not according to a reader's whim or fluctuating choice. Such is the conservative's belief.

Conservatism, I have insisted, should be informed conservatism. The point is stressed because a nervous loyalty has sought too often to steady the ark of God with clumsy hands. It has tended to defend indefensible positions, narrow the legitimate area for difference of opinion and to adopt over-dogmatic attitudes, especially in matters of eschatology, wherein a wide field is open for devout interpretation. Some conservatives, impatient with the transient and sometimes irresponsible theorizings of scholarship, have been, with equal irresponsibility, critical of scholarship generally.

Informed conservatism welcomes all the light which learned research can throw on Scripture. It is no devotee of literalism, not committed to Ussher's dates, to a 'futurist' view of the Apocalypse, or to the text of the King James Version. Its view of Scripture can absorb all genuine discovery, although it has sometimes failed to demonstrate that confidence, and opposed where it should have adapted.

Consider, for example, the 'documentary theory' of the Pentateuch. From Wellhausen onwards notable absurdities were perpetrated by those who shredded the books of Moses, and biblical scholarship has long since repudiated such folly. Could anything be more outrageous folly than the oddity of the Polychrome Bible?

It was right, in the face of such attack, for conservatives, for example, to defend the Mosaic authorship and to combat the pernicious thesis that the Jewish faith had its origin in superstition and forgery. But the question of documents embedded in the text in no way impugned the traditional authorship or the sanctity of the books. How unlikely it would have been had Abraham, the heir of a literary society, had no written records of his own or earlier religious experience. How unlikely would it have been had Joseph, with the scribes of Egypt at his call, composed no record

29

of his life. Indeed, is it not possible in the English version to pick that point where the terse style dictated by the clay tablet gives place to the expansive style of the writer on papyrus? And does it not add to the authority of the documents, if Moses, putting them into final form, looked upon them with such reverence that he could not bring himself to change a word? My point is this. Conservatism would have demonstrated greater dignity and respect for truth than some of its exponents did, had it stood fast for the authenticity of the documents, but accepted with gratitude any discoveries which threw light on their composition.

The fact must be faced that, over vital and lamentable years in the latter years of the last century, and the early years of this, conservative thought neglected scholarship. In some cases, finding itself, of its own act, lacking in scholarship, it took to despising it. The reasons were three. It was the great age of preaching. The pulpit was the goal of those who sought to serve, and the pulpit is a hard master and exacting. Neither Spurgeon nor Parker, Moody nor Talmadge, were great scholars. Admittedly, R. W. Dale and J. H. Jowett were fine scholars as well as magnificent preachers, but Torrey was the first scholarly evangelist of global reputation.

Preaching, too, was forwarded at the expense of scholarship by a widely proclaimed and accepted eschatology which, Thessalonian fashion, saw a Second Advent so imminently near, that plans of preparation involving years of study seemed a confession of unbelief. I vividly remember a wild-eyed youth advancing precisely that argument against my own University program in 1922. I believed, since I believed Christ, in his second intrusion into history, but I also believed what he said about the mystery of that climax. Thirdly, the world was opening with incomparable opportunities for missionary enterprise, and ability was drained off into these wide and effective channels in a fashion which went far to strip the Church at home of leadership in thought.

Meanwhile the liberals, not so devoted to missionary

enterprise, sceptical of orthodox eschatology, without the evangelical urge to preach, gave their energy and enterprise to church politics and theological teaching. In a word they practically monopolized the schools, and such a triumph introduces a time-lag of half a century, even when promptly countered, for the teacher has his pupils who bear the marks of their classroom through life. And the move was not promptly countered. One must not forget men like Orr and Denney, whom I have mentioned with gratitude, and later Machen and a few like them, but the fact remains that liberal theology dug its trenches deep in strategic places, and is still far from being dislodged. The persecution of J. G. Machen of Princeton, one powerful conservative of the twenties, was a sign of the times.

The nineteenth century was a sceptical age, obsessed with the idea of progress. In fact, man had never moved so fast. Each year saw new invention, the dating and supersession of the long used and long familiar. In Anglo-Saxon lands industrial progress was unbroken and spectacular, not without reflection in society. The restless questing for something better produced not only multiplying invention but improved conditions. Science grew apace, and as rapid new discovery found prompt application in the improved amenities of life, the vision of a material millennium became, among the favored few, an article of faith.

In addition, progress found a ready-made philosophy in Darwinism. Darwin put forward his theory of evolution as biological hypothesis. It was promptly hailed as a synthesis of truth, applied to morals, religion, philology, and all else in the view of man. This transfer was unwarranted and indeed absurd. In religion it spawned major and reprehensible error. And it was met less by reasoned rebuttal, than by shrill protest.

Conditioned rapidly to think in terms of evolution, and in an environment which daily, until the Edwardian afterglow, illustrated the passing of the lesser for the greater, and the growing complexity of convenience and wealth, thinkers generally looked on progress as self-evident. It was the age of *Locksley Hall*, unshadowed by Tennyson's later disillusionment, of Wells' first optimism without hint of his final despair. Some never doubted. 'The flower of humanity,' said Horder, 'will blossom one day into a state of which no man on earth can imagine the majesty.' 'Progress therefore,' concluded the irritatingly pontifical Herbert Spencer, 'is not an accident. It is a part of Nature.' John Addington Symonds wrote his poem 'These things shall be' in the same climate, and might have been surprised today to find it included in some hymnals.

In short everything was getting better and better, and the favored middle class in Britain and America who gave noisiest voice for the world at large, failed to realize how few they were who ate the fruits of ramifying invention. Mr. Podsnap had only to look at less favored peoples to see how glorious was the day, how superior to yesterday, and how certain was a glorious tomorrow. It was odd that the concept survived the First World War. I remember hearing in Liverpool in 1924, during my wanderyear, an ardent young Methodist preach on the text: 'They journeyed towards the sunrising.' Had we not the League of Nations? How infinitely sad, it seems, from this end of the century.

What has this to do with religion? This. The notion was ingrained that everything which was of yesterday was out-of-date. The Bible belonged to the age of the coach, the bow and arrow, of sail, of tyranny. Religion, like the rest, and all its records, must have 'evolved.' It was so easy for thinking so warped to seize the suggestion that the Bible grew piecemeal, from smaller to larger, with clarifying thought, as man, noble, upward-striving man, won loftier concepts of the divine. How favorable the climate was for Wellhausen and his avid train of imitators is obvious.

Such jubilant iconoclasm found its most foolish extravagances in the German universities, were the very requirements of the Ph.D. degree pandered to irreverent, insincere, and exhibitionist attacks on all tradition. Before the onslaught the Church trembled. Some bright minds were lost. Matthew Arnold, son of a great Christian, became a melancholy agnostic, and he was one of many. Others rejected the scholarship which had turned so hostile, and in a passion of pure faith plunged into evangelism with vast reward among the industrial poor, but smaller contact with the educated. A generation, perhaps two, was unevangelized over large tracts of its more cultured and educated strata. It was at this time that university scepticism struck such deep roots. Others set out to salvage some rags of religion, and an abbreviated Bible, from the wreck around them which, to their hasty eyes, seemed complete. Arnold was more logical, who knew rationalism when he saw it, and withdrew.

The crossless Christianity so common in the early years of this century, was the invention of the Victorian liberals who were first daunted by the dogmatism of radical biblical scholarship. It was optimistic on evolutionary principles, turned Christ into a crusading knight, expended its energy on social problems, and, for the more spiritually-minded, substituted a personal mysticism for the lost authority of an inspired Bible.

The *Oxford Dictionary of the Christian Church* spoke of liberalism as an attitude which 'until recently', that is until the middle fifties, appeared to be gaining acceptance; liberalism, in face, as I said, survived the First World War. The thirties and the second global conflict were its death blow.

Why? Liberalism had no personal message. This is the situation which faced me as an earnest young Christian, with such a challenge. Honesty should have realized that it was rationalism. Churches which preached its attenuated Christianity were obviously failing early in this century, save where a dynamic preacher or leader infused his own spirit into the organization. Harry Emerson Fosdick has been a notable example of such a personal success. The pews were, in general, emptying, and a religion built largely of the Christian ethic, without dynamism, sanctions, and external authority, was clearly failing, not only to convert the fading rose-coloured world but to hold its first enthusiasts.

Furthermore the haste of the conclusions was being exposed. The exciting new science of archaeology, in both classical and biblical scholarship, was making Victorian speculation appear increasingly ridiculous, and establishing the worth and validity of tradition, a conviction which, from a classical training, I had never abandoned. The ancient records proved astonishingly reliable, as discovery on discovery confirmed the statements of ancient historians, and demonstrated the folly of recent theorizing. The story of the 'Tubingen School,' and its favorite interpretation of John's Gospel, so ludicrously toppled by one small archaeological find, is an illustration too long to detail here. Anyway, it is notorious.

Nor was the state of the world any encouragement, as we passed into the sombre prelude to war and that ordeal itself, to the optimism which was necessarily a part of a religion which leaned so heavily on evolutionary views of the Bible. The Bible diagnosis of man was so obviously correct. Scientific progress which led to Hiroshima seemed somehow discredited, and human depravity proved final comment on the simple-minded conclusion that a glorious race was arising because steam had replaced sail, and man had learned to fly.

Honest liberals realized that the game was up. Their message was irrelevant, or if relevant to the minds of constitutional enthusiasts, had nothing in it which could be cogently, evangelistically or authoritatively preached. The test of the pulpit was decisive. The theological schools became an ordeal, a sort of testing by heat, a Mithraic initiation, through which the would-be preacher passed, shutting his ears, if the figure may be varied, if so be he might carry some conviction through to the pulpit. Like something prehistoric, liberalism still clings to such platforms, and ardent youth still in some quarters has such a gauntlet of the mind to run on the way to the pulpit steps. I think one of the saddest statements I have ever read came from a group of theological students from one major liberal school headed: 'They have taken away my Lord, and I know not where they have laid him.'

Disillusioned liberals, who were still of an age and temper to think, reacted variously. Some followed logic and sought less compromising ways of life. I had a respected teacher of that ilk. Few carried Browning's Bishop Blougram into later years than those in which the perspicacious poet wrote – the generality of churchmen surely earn that confidence. Remember?

> *Observe, my friend,*
> *Such as you know me, I am free to say,*
> *In these hard latter days which hamper one,*
> *Myself by no immoderate exercise*
> *Of intellect and learning, and the tact*
> *To let external forces work for me,*
> *Bid the street's stones be bread, and they are bread,*
> *Bid Peter's creed, or, rather, Hildebrand's,*
> *Exalt me o'er my fellows in the world*
> *And make my life an ease and joy and pride . . .*

Others, remote from such patent and rare insincerity, sought outlet in social work. Lloyd Douglas, whose biography is a document of liberalism's bankruptcy, passed through such a phase, before his spirit found an outlet, and the clear beginnings of a pathway back, in religious novel-writing. Others, held by a vested interest marched on to form and to expound various philosophical forms of 'religion', and at final worst, to beget the 'God is dead' doctrines of the sixties. There were others, and they are world-wide, who genuinely returned to a conservative faith and found it satisfying.

Others, and for them I reserve more sympathetic attention, invented 'neo-orthodoxy.' It is difficult to define the term, for its shades of meaning are many. I exclude from the category the exponents of 'double talk,' who accept orthodox doctrine in a symbolic sense, and preach with private meaning. The simple audience hears ancient truth. The preacher sees from the pulpit an horizon of his own behind their heads. Euripides did something like that with old myths in his drama. With old myths it did not matter. I speak here of a simpler neo-orthodoxy, and more sincere.

Broadly speaking, the neo-orthodox churchman does hold and seeks to proclaim the great doctrines which the conservative has never abandoned, and which events have demonstrated to be the only effective and preachable form of Christianity. He holds such doctrines by faith, and finds their confirmation in their potency to convict and save, and in the conviction of his inner experience. What he lacks is an authoritative Bible. Generally, he has been unable, while accepting so much else, to abandon the liberal view of Scripture. He finds himself in tune with those who wrote the record, but that record remains no more than the corpus of man's insights, the story of his battling towards a clearer concept of truth. This is not to say that the conservative denies progress in Scripture, but it is for him progressive relevation, and the record, though given through the mind of man and in man's speech, is overruled, in the conservative's belief, and invested with authority.

But I have said enough on the theme. This book, as its title gives clear notice, is autobiographical, and I presumed to make it such because I realised that my six decades of Christian profession have seen some sweeping tides of religious thought. It was not serene travelling to tread a conservative path, as a younger Christian, if integrity and honesty of mind meant what they did to me. I could not accept a divided pattern of thought, I could not believe that truth could be differently applied in different compartments of thought. I would not accept that faith was an outrage against reason. If Tertullian said: 'It is certain because it is impossible', Tertullian was a fool.

I chose conservatism because I saw no alternative. I was aware of all that stance involved. With the enormous growth of Biblical scholarship, the position has been most abundantly vindicated and I am glad I kept a cool head as that vindication came, and I made my own contributions to it. It remains to me now to pick up some themes touched on in passing, to illustrate and to expand.

4: Half a century with John

It was my very good fortune to approach the study of the New Testament by way of the Greek and Latin Classics. Heavily preoccupied in my early University teaching career with two great literatures and the dozen skills and disciplines associated with them, I learned how to appraise an ancient document, to place it and accommodate it in its time and situation, to scrutinise with an informed eye what was written about it in books and learned periodicals, and to apply with scrupulous regard for evidence the exacting canons of literary and historical criticism.

Two perfectly simple lessons were simultaneously set for me to learn. One begins the study of any piece of literature first by reading it thoroughly, and establishing what the writer had to say, his purpose in writing and his mode of communication. In the second place one respects ancient tradition and does not reject it without the most compelling reasons.

Such simple principles I found, when I at last had time to turn in detail to Biblical criticism, were not notable among many scholars in that sphere. This is the gravest of faults in the curricula and teaching methods of many theological colleges. Before students have opportunity to know with thoroughness the substance of their texts, and what has been accepted fact about them, they are primed with a point of view, a too often irrelevant or perverse philosophy, and a too commonly deviant theology. So many institutions of Biblical learning, over the period of which I have complained, captured and conditioned the minds of those they taught, before they had a chance to hear or to consider any possible alternative view, or even the basic texts.

Reading Classics, teaching its surviving works, keeping up with relevant publication in English, French, German, Italian, it came about that I began the teaching of the New Testament as an extracurricular activity with little more than the Greek text, usually from the *Expositor's Greek Testament* in my hand. I suppose I have, in the course of half a century, lectured through the text of the Fourth Gospel fifty or sixty times. I thus knew a great book as a document of literature, long before I paid detailed attention to the large amount of liberal comment written about it. When I came to do so, I was aghast at the perverse, prejudiced, pernicious nonsense I found written.

I had come quite naturally to know John with the curious intimacy with which a student of a particular author becomes acquainted with the personality of the man over whose writings he had long pored. I touched on that experience of intimacy and understanding with the Roman poets Lucretius, Vergil and Catullus, and with the Greek Euripides, on whom I have lectured and written busily. But in no case more than with John, the apostle.

The acute visual and audial memory of the man (a trait which, sometimes distressingly, I share with him) is a notable demonstration of personality. Glance through the book. Chapter One with its eighteen introductory verses, summing up and containing the whole message of the Bible, shows how remarkably the fisherman of Galilee, like his friend Peter, had become a citizen of two worlds. It was due no doubt to the tutelage of Paul. Here was the Intelligence Behind Phenomena expressing itself in Christ, as it had shown itself in Creation. Swiftly and decisively, John turns to his namesake, the Baptiser, leader of the most remarkable 'prophetic' revival, as Christ himself said, that the land had ever seen. For his special purpose, as the century entered its last decade, John needed the desert preacher's witness, for tall heresies were abroad. But observe how John achieves his purpose in a few swift pen strokes of description . . .

Unable to grasp a striking feature of their history, that sudden inruption into corrupt urban religion of a voice from field or wilderness, an Amos, maybe, or an Elijah, the proud hierarchy sent an ill-briefed team to investigate John, as they similarly sent, as Mark tell us, to Capernaum to report on the Lord.

'Who are you?' they call from the river bank. John was busy in one of the clear pools which lie twenty feet below the packed yellow silt and mud of the lower Jordan valley today. With a minimum of words he replies: 'I am not the Messiah.'

'What then?' they ask, 'Are you Elijah?' 'I am not,' he snaps back. 'Are you the prophet?' (Alluding to Malachi's oracle). Realising that they had gone too far beyond courtesy with their neuter pronoun (*What* then?), they continue. 'Who then? We want to give a reply to those who sent us. What do you say about yourself?' (They were alarmed at the thought of an impatient Caiaphas). Thus properly addressed, John quotes Isaiah (Curious, is it not, that a few miles away in the library of Qumran lay a most beautiful roll of Isaiah?). 'I? The voice of one crying in the wilderness, Prepare the way of the Lord . . .'

How intensely vivid it all is, with such economy of speech. And the whole incident (it was in the Jordanian Bethany) is linked with the appearance of the Messiah, and the Messiah in the character he so often assumes in John, who knew him more deeply than the rest. John the Baptist had identified him at the place of baptism, and the evangelist had noted the anquished repetition of 'And I did not know him.' Magnificently, he sends two of his close followers to go with the One 'whose shoe he was not worthy to take off,' and in sequence of events comes Nathaniel, despising the little town of Nazareth, and cool to his friend Philip's cautious approach: 'The one of whom Moses wrote about in the law, the prophets too, we have found him, Jesus, son of Joseph, from Nazareth.' Philip knew that the weakest word was 'Nazareth.' One sees such detail in the Greek text. He kept 'Nazareth' till the end, vainly.

Unwillingly Nathaniel comes, and is puzzled by Christ's

warm commendation until the fig-tree is mentioned, when in striking haste Nathaniel warmly acknowledges him. Why? Something happened under that fig-tree, with which Christ's mind coupled so uncannily, that Nathaniel's surrender was immediate. 'You believe because I said I saw you under the fig-tree? You'll see things more remarkable than this. Truly you will see heaven opened, and God's angels going up and down upon the Son of Man.'

Was 'the Israelite indeed' thinking, as he prayed in his shady place of prayer, of the lost path between earth and heaven, no ziggurat stairway such as Jacob saw between man and his God, no true prophet for centuries, a conquered trodden land? 'Dear God when will the way again be open?' And now someone says: 'I know about that prayer. The way, I tell you, is now open again. I am Jacob's ladder, the pathway of God's self-revealing, the road of man's ascent to God.' John trusted his readers to see his point. He wrote like that. So must we read.

Look at Chapter Two. It is always good to remember that ancient books were not divided into chapters and verses. They were simply books, commonly determined by the length of a roll of papyrus, which seems to have had an accepted practicable maximum of twenty-eight feet. On the other hand, though our divisions are, on the whole fairly felicitous, they do, on occasion, blur a sequence . . .

John passes on to the homeliest of themes, a country wedding just along the ridge at Cana north of Nazareth. John's simple realism and quiet evocation of atmosphere is apparent again. The wedding atmosphere is felt with Mary, an elder relative, perhaps, doing her best to help. When a crisis looms she turned to her son. He had never failed her in life's emergencies. 'They have no wine', she whispers. 'Mother', he protests, 'what is that to you and me?' (This is the correct rendering) 'This is not my occasion.' She hurries off saying to the servants: 'Do exactly what he says.' There is no theology about the story, only simple truth down to the best man's poor joke about keeping the cheap wine until the guests were less perceptive. Poor lad, it was probably his first speech. But how real it all is, as real as the very different scene in the cattle-yard into which the crude and avaricious priestly corporation had converted the lovely temple court. Only a figure standing there, twisting in his hands a snatch of cattle halters, left lying in the straw and dung when the beasts were led away. A figure standing, looking sternly round. Panic! Someone remembers Malachi's picture. Fumbling control, a broken pen. Sheep and oxen stampeding for the gate amid a confusion of tumbled tables. The truth breaks on the mind if the story is read, as a real narrative. He did nothing, did not move, never used his bunch of cords. Otherwise he would have been arrested but they had no charge to lay. Exasperated, they questioned his 'authority', and had an enigmatic reply.

John ends the chapter by a remark on the Lord's strange insight into human personality. 'He knew what was in man.' As, for example, a leading Pharisee. (Ignore the chapter division). He came by night, not necessarily through fear. It was wisdom not to be openly associated with the Galilean movement until he was convinced. He was '*the* teacher of Israel', for all the obstinacy of the translators in rendering the definite article by an indefinite, a fault to be found in other places. Academics, such as Nicodemus, like to be convinced, and have every right to such predilection. The conversation can only be understood as an interplay of minds, behind a screen of language. Nicodemus began with a most polite exordium, and was annoyed when the Lord drove straight to the point. He had come to ask about 'the Kingdom.' Perhaps the new prophet had some enlightenment. As though weary of this common material misconception, Christ spoke, almost sharply, of the Kingdom which mattered, that of Heaven and God's rule.

Nicodemus knew what he meant. A man whose whole thought was permeated and infused with the words of the Old Testament, must have thought immediately of the Thirty-Sixth chapter of Ezekiel with its promise of a heart renewed, a regeneration of the personality, a changed outlook, as soon as the mention of a rebirth was made. If proof of such interchange of unspoken ideas is needed it is the sudden intrusion of the reference to the unfettered wind, a metaphor for God's Spirit, since in both the languages of the Bible, the same word is used for 'wind' and 'spirit'. And the Pharisee would think immediately of the grisly dream which follows in the Old Testament book. It is a valley of stark death where some tiny valiant rearguard had tried to stop the flow of Babylon's armour, which advanced on the doomed land. A 'beqaa', or valley plain, was their highway, and hoof and wheel had ridden down the desperate defenders. It was a ghastly picture of trampled, ruined Israel. Such bones could as likely live as Israel itself. The War Graves Commission in 1921, found our Anzac dead lying thus under Sari Bair, the whitened remnants of our last charge in 1915.

Nicodemus was attentive now. 'We speak that which we do know', said the Lord and they both did. The message seemed to come from the ending of the prophet's dream of Death Beqaa, that the bones of Israel could only live if God gave them life. But must one wait he asked, for such wonder to 'come about', until such time as God chose to breathe in such salvation? Was grace, revival, rebirth sovereign action, uninfluenced by man at all?

The strange double-level conversation went on. 'No', the Lord answers, taking his fascinated listener back to Moses in the asp-ridden wilderness, 'those who looked lived, and soon there will be an uplifted stake again, and all would be back to the personal response of individual Israelites like you, Nicodemus.' That is how Nicodemus in the end got his answer. The Lord spoke to 'what was in him.' And that is how, as I read and understood, I myself found the meaning of a chapter whch had puzzled me since boyhood, when I read it in the little Bible with the creased leather cover on my desk by my bed on the little farm. It was moving revelation.

John goes on to comment, for this chapter is in three clear divisions containing some noble words. But this is not a commentary on John, merely a rapid sketch of the vast humanity of the book, the clarity of the writer's person showing through its interwoven themes, the unity of its account so obviously written by one who saw and recorded, and read unencumbered.

But the story of the Pharisee has set John's mind working on that theme: 'He knew what was in man.' Consider another encounter at the other end of the social scale. He was under some compulsion which puzzled them (a state in which they often found themselves, as we do, by his doings) to go through Samaria. They left him seated on a well-curb, on which, if the roadblocks which man puts between man and life's living waters are penetrated, you may sit still today and sip the purest water in Israel. It is near tense Nablus.

With the same realism John tells of the Samaritan woman from Sychar. There is a little known play of Edmond Rostand, who died in the great Influenza Epidemic of 1918, on the theme. *Cyrano de Bergerac*, and the less well-known *L'Aiglon* and *Chantecler*, so monopolise his stage that Rostand's lesser work is sometimes forgotten. But *La Samaritaine* is a brief and quite moving rendering of John Chapter 4.

He is at rest on the well-curb, and sees her coming, beautiful and defiant, one hand on her hip, and one steadying the amphora on her head, looking just like the two-handled jar itself, he remarks in soliloquy, and just as empty. He asks for a drink. 'You a Jew, asking a drink of me, a woman, and a Samaritan,?' to use both John's words and Rostand's. 'Jews don't use the same cups as the Samaritans,' she sneers.

She lets the jar down, and brings it carefully up filled to the brim. She stands it on the well-curb tauntingly. 'See, rabbi', the dramatist makes her say, 'it is so full, and the water is so pure that you would think it contained nothing at all.' 'So', he replies, 'is everyone who is filled with the water I can give.' A beautiful thought. The 'fulness of the Holy Spirit' is not marked by embullience, noise, turmoil. It takes and commands the whole personality, and yet is a Presence shaped by the container.

But leave Rostand to his beautiful little drama. We are seeking John, the old bishop of Ephesus, and his chapter

43

itself is dramatic enough. The woman is full of bravado, but would not have been drawing her water at midday, had she not been in truth too fragile to face the other women of the town. She relished this chance to insult a Jew. Indeed, presented as they were once with the opportunity to bring their faith to a sorry remnant of refugees restored by the Assyrians to Samaria, the Jews had rejected the Samaritans as unclean, and spawned a hate which still endured, and which the Jews had provoked.

But no flame of wrath was struck from the man sitting on the well. He merely spoke a word about another water which quenches the soul's thirst. 'A deep well', the woman counters drily. (And it is deep, a great feat of ancient engineering). 'Nor have you a dipper. How comes this living water?' Pause. One must learn to read John's narrative. Read slowly here. He simply looks at her. His look could penetrate, as they found in the temple-court, as Peter too was one day to find. She cannot stand the silence, and blurts: 'Are you greater than our father Jacob who gave us this well?' (Slightest emphasis on 'our' and 'us') . . . No answer. '. . . and drank of it himself . . . and his sons . . . and his cattle.' Staccato. She can think of no more to say. He continued with more about a mysterious water of life. That was another object John had in writing. He was, it will be noticed by a careful reader, setting great sayings in their context of events. His water would satisfy. Indeed it would turn one who drank it into a fountain of life, not a mere container like the jar on the well-curb, but an overflowing spring. Awkwardly, and flippant now because of her awkwardness, she rushes on, 'Give me this water, sir', she says 'so that I shall not thirst, nor keep coming here to draw.'

He sees the time is ripe to drive deep into her damaged personality. 'Go and call your man', he says. Oddly she cannot lie. 'I haven't one.' 'A true word that', he answers, 'you've had five men and the man you are now living with is not yours. Yes, you told the truth.' A blow to the heart. She rallies and sets out to flaunt a theological argument about the Jewish and Samaritan claims to possess the holy place. Who is right? He brushes it all aside. God is spirit, unbound by time and locality. 'Oh well, the Messiah will settle it.' 'I am the Messiah', he says. Can anyone doubt the authenticity of that conversation? The woman makes off, her water pot left on the well, and the disciples come back. He puzzles them as he always did, speaking now of mystic food, as he spoke of mystic water. But he was waiting, his eyes on the hill-top, the road's bend. And sure enough they came, the splash of white as the garments of the eastern crowd appeared in sight. 'What was that tune you were singing as you came along this morning? "Only a four-month, and then comes the harvest." Well look up, it is here now. I made you fishers of men. Now you can be reapers too.'

It is John at his best, his vivid recall of word and event, his touch of drama. 'He knew what was in man', and John, as no other, knew Christ, and was specially dear to him for his swift insights, 'the disciple whom Jesus loved.' I came innocently to the story and read it as a page of vivid Greek. I did not know then that it was a strong asseveration of some critics that 'Christ never specifically claimed to be the Messiah.' Of course, of course, if that must be the starting point of historical investigation, the story of the Sychar well must, indeed, be banished from the corpus of evidence, but a classics student would not act so stupidly. He would begin with his page of simple Greek, and it cannot be ignored.

One could go on all through John's narrative in the same way showing the consistency of the portraiture of Christ by the last alive who remembered him. Look at the scene of the sad crowd by the Bethesda pool, possibly, in the light of the passage we examined as an exercise in the 'lower criticism', a cruel fraud of the priests, and until 1932 dismissed by the 'higher criticism' as an allegory of the law and the gospel with 'five porches' as a Pentateuch! (The pool, with the proper number of porches is now excavated so this piece of nonsense has joined its fellows in the appropriate academic dust-bin). But observe Christ's first question. 'Do you want to be well?' People can adapt to horror.

People can find disability profitable. John saw the Lord's point and unerringly recorded it. The whole incident, along with the cattle-market story, was another in the sequence of the clash with the Sadducees.

Turn to John's account of the feeding of the hungry crowd across the Lake of Galilee, sitting like 'garden beds, garden beds', as Peter told Mark, fumbling for the right word. Observe the little scene. He speaks to Philip whom he knows will have it all worked out. Yes, 'two hundred denarii for a slice apiece.' Andrew jokes: 'There's a lad here with five barley rolls and a couple of smoked fish.' Finding that the Lord turns with interest, he weakly adds: 'Not much for such a crowd' . . . So very natural, like the two incidents in the next chapter, the poignant little situation in which his own brothers reject him, and the truly amazing acceptance by the Sanhedrin of the excuse of their officers for not arresting him: 'No one speaks like this man.' He had dismissed them with a look. The priests knew the sort of look. They had seen it. They had watched silent crowds listening to him. The picture of him comes through, as it is reflected in the faces of others. In bitter anger they dismiss Nicodemus, who, no coward, tried a dignified defence, as a 'Galilean'.

In Chapter Eight, who, with any sensitivity to literature, could doubt the authenticity of the story of the woman? They drag her in. 'Now, rabbi', they snarl, 'Moses was clear on this issue. But, of course, you have your own ideas about Moses.' Silence, his old device while the reality of his presence filled the scene. He did not even ask where the man was (She was 'taken in the very act'). He made marks on the sand at his feet. What? A name? A date? He looked up. It was that steady look again. 'Let the one without sin throw first', he said.

The story of the blind man in the next chapter in another classic of eye-witness reporting. John, clearly, had access to the deliberative quarters of the priests. There was less privacy in those days. Folk went in and out. John was known in the house of Caiaphas or Annas. Perhaps he was a selling agent for the family fishing-business on Galilee, but can it be doubted, provided that the story is carefully read, that the writer saw and heard what he records? It is vibrantly real in the Greek text.

Read the chapter. John has another saying of Christ in mind: 'I am the light of the world.' In fact John has the imagery of light and darkness in the forefront of his thinking. There was much talk among the cultists whom he was writing specifically to refute about the 'enlightened', those who held characteristic elitist doctrines, and the saying brought to his mind a blind beggarman who was the victim of a special inquisition in the priestly court. Sitting in his wretchedness at some city gate, he was seen by the Lord's men, fresh perhaps from a petty theological disputation with the scribes, a timely theme, they thought for such a question. Blindness, of course, like all the manifold afflictions of life, was, it was thought, a result of sin. Was it his own sin, seeing he was born blind, sin perhaps, as some would maintain, prenatally committed? Or rather was it a parent's misdeeds, visited upon the next generation? In either case it quenched pity. If suffering was merited, why then commiserate?

'Rabbi,' they ask, 'who sinned, this man or his parents, that he should be blind from his birth?' The reply was sharp and intense: 'Neither this man sinned nor his parents — but that the works of God may be shown in him, it becomes us to do the works of the one who sent me while we have the light of day. Night comes when none can work. I am the world's light while I am in the world.'

Observe the correct punctuation, which translators who forget that John did not supply such aides, consistently avoid, making God the author of the man's malady, in order that, after all those weary years, God might demonstrate in Christ his power to heal. God is not like that.

The Lord did a strange thing. The blind man probably believed the common superstition that the spittle of a good man had healing properties. He met the poor creature, as he meets us, on the humble level of his faith, and smeared his eyelids with dust and spittle. 'Go and wash in the Siloam pool,' he said. He went off and washed himself and came back seeing, to the amazement of his parents, and others who had seen him on his mat begging. Was it the same man? Was it someone like him? 'It is I, all right', he said. 'How then do you see?' 'A man named Jesus, made clay, anointed my eyes, and told me to go to the Siloam and wash. I did, I washed, I saw.' 'Where is he, this man?' 'I don't know', he said.

They take the one-time blind man into the Pharisees — it was the Sabbath when Jesus did his deed, and some no doubt felt that those dignitaries should know. The Pharisees asked him in their turn how he regained his sight. The man was wary now. No one could sit for a lifetime, sightlessly begging, and not become wise in the world's evil ways. He mentions no name, and in a studied economy of words replied: 'He put clay on my eyes, I washed myself and I can see.' Some of the Pharisees intoned: 'This man is not from God, because he does not keep the Sabbath.' Others, less bigoted (one would hope Nicodemus was among them), said: 'How can a sinner do such miracles?' And they fell into argument, an uncomely scene.

They said to the blind man: 'What do you say about him, seeing he gave you sight?' He replied: 'He is a voice of God.' Confusion reigned. 'The Jews' (John seems to use the term, Galilean-fashion, to designate hard-core city Jewry) professing scepticism, called in the man's aged parents, and addressed a question to them. One can almost hear the pompous, condescending tone. 'This is your son, who, you say, was born blind? How then does he now see?' The old folk confine themselves cautiously in fact: 'We know that this is our son, and that he was born blind. How he now sees we do not know, or who gave him sight we do not know. Ask him. He is a grown man. He will speak for himself.' Thus the parents, as John adds, afraid of 'the Jews', who had already laid it down that whoever confessed him the Messiah should be excommunicated, a traumatic fate.

Unwisely, they called the man in again, and made their solemn pronouncement: 'Give glory to God. We know that this man is a sinner.' The 'we know' nettled the brave fellow. He replied: 'As to his being a sinner, I do not know. One fact I do know. I was blind and now I see.' More unwisely still, they opened the cross-examination again: 'What did he do to you? How did he give you your sight?' 'I told you and you did not listen. Why do you want to hear again?' And with a flash of brilliant testimony, he added: 'Surely you too don't wish to become his disciples?'

They reviled him, and fell foolishly into argument: 'You are his disciple. We are Moses' disciples. We know that God spoke to Moses. As for this man we do not know where he comes from.' That fatal 'we know' again! Did the man, daring a further impertinence, repeat the pompous verb twice with the faintest mimicry of the spokesman's tone? 'Yes, here is an amazing thing, that you do not know where he comes from, and he gave me sight. We know that God does not hear sinners, but if a man be a worshipper of God and does his will, him God hears. It is something unheard of that one should give sight to a man born blind. If this man were not from God he could do nothing.' They answered: 'You, born utterly in sin, you, trying to teach us?' And they put him out. Read with proper emphasis on verbs and pronouns, and catch the reality of the angry confrontation. It is deliciously told. No one made this conversation out of nothing, for some fraudulent end. Fiction was not a developed form of literature in those days, much less among the proletariat. Much less was this 'myth', even in the misleading fashion in which liberal critics misuse the word myth. It was brilliant reporting.

The touching little scene which follows and closes the chapter was beautifully dramatised by Dorothy Sayers over forty years ago. The meeting of Christ with Jacob, the blind man, standing in wonder at the moon, is a moving passage. But then, the distinguished dramatist had read the story from the text. She wore out three Greek Testaments in making her dramatised story of Christ. It is necessary for all understanding first to read the story with care, and ask if it could be true. That is what Dorothy Sayers did. So did I. So should everyone.

A correct conclusion cannot be reached if the investigator

insists on beginning with a false assumption. That was the fault of Ernest Renan. The great French Hebraist, penetrating critic in many literary and philosophical spheres, was known to me because I studied him, in senior student days, when I took one of my two Master's degrees, with Honours in French. That is when I encountered his *Life of Jesus*. I shall return later to this experience. I was fascinated by his beautiful language, but saw, even in those days of youthful Christianity, his two faults. He stated that he would consider no event historical or true, if it contained the miraculous in any form. I could also see, what his contemporaries saw and assailed, how his mastery of the French language enabled him to 'clothe disbelief in the garb, tones and phrases of belief.' In some quarters liberal scholarship has made such practice a fine art. Renan's initial determination survived an archaeological tour of Palestine in which he confessed that 'the striking agreement of the texts and places, the marvellous harmony of the evangelical idea, and of the country which served it as a framework were to me a revelation . . . a fifth Gospel, disfigured, though still legible.' How true, but what a pity that a spirit so alive, so warm in admiration for Jesus the man, so sincerely sensitive to the power of his spoken words, should have approached the written records with such self-inflicted blindness, such hobbling of prejudice.

My reading of Renan did me no harm. I could already see that the very frankness of his avowed attitude closed the path to what I was about to discover in the documents, but I mention him because the most crucially testing chapter in John's narrative lies ahead. It tells of the raising of Lazarus.

Chapter Eleven, could, of course, find no historical acceptance with the 'demythologists.' The very name, Lazarus, was discussed by Renan's successors. It was not a possible name. Even with my smattering of Hebrew (I have never known the language well) it occurred to me when I turned with close attention to John, that 'Lazarus' was precisely what Greek would make of the common Hebrew name of Eliezer, Abraham's servant, the second son of

Moses and one of Ezra's envoys. Lazarus was Eliezer, and in recent years all the place and personal names in John stand archaeologically attested. The question is, however, whether the same style of writing which functioned so con-vincingly in Chapter Nine, changed two chapters later.

John begins as he began before, with a matter-of-fact turn of phrase. A touch of personality peeps out. He was a little weary of hearing Luke's tale of Martha and Mary turned so often to Martha's disadvantage, and subtly corrected it: 'Jesus loved Martha and her sister and Lazarus.' To be sure he had just mentioned Mary, but observe the gentle precedence given to the vigorous Martha. Observe, too, Martha's character, and her sister's in the story. Martha is in firm control, Mary broken and immobile in her despair, Martha's frank horror at the exposure of a dead body, her brother's too, left in the tomb for more than the three days through which, by Jewish superstition, the spirit was thought to linger in the place of death. Note Jesus. By an inspired division, whoever versed and paragraphed the story made one verse of 'Jesus wept.' He felt to the depth of his being the mental agony of the sisters, and in spite of what he knew he was about to do, he communed lovingly with their shattering sorrow.

Was not this the same John who had written with sharp and vivid memory of word and of event, whom we have followed thus far? If so why should we dub him a liar, a dupe or a maker of myth when, in the same simple language, he describes how he saw a stone rolled from a tomb-front, and the dead occupant stagger into the sunlight, tangled in his grave-clothes? So stands the matter, and no more need be said save to point out the dilemma of unbelief. And it need not be said that those whom John then and now convinced, themselves have not wrestled with the problem. The chief actor in the scene was Christ. Believe that Christ was what he said he was, believe that, if there is a God who made the laws which interweave the universe, he can also operate in areas of law which no human investigation into the phenomena of creation has been able to penetrate, and then the difficulties which the modern mind encounters assume their proper proportion, and come within reach of faith. So, at least, it seemed to me when, as a young Christian, I read and read again the bald narrative of events.

Then the tense story of Chapter Thirteen . . . John tells of the prelude to the Last Supper, but also records the sequel to events described in Mark and Luke. That sad walk up from Jericho with the Lord striding, seemingly alone, ahead, the sound of feet behind him and the crude, unfeeling clamour of James and John for the prime seats in 'the Kingdom', which they were sure, in spite of weeks of instruction all the way down from Caesarea Philippi, they were certain now he must establish. The tension was palpable in the room. He rose from the table, knotted a towel around his waist and began to wash the disciples' feet. 'You do not now understand what I am doing, but the time will come when you will.' He came to Peter who burst out: 'You will certainly not wash my feet – ever.' 'Unless I do', said Christ mysteriously, 'you are none of mine.' And Peter, so characteristically: 'Not my feet only but my hands and my head.'

He took his seat again, and he spoke again, on the meaning of what he had done. He told of betrayal on the part of one of them. Peter signed to John, who was at Christ's side, to ask who it was. He answered in an action. He dipped some bread in the dish, or rolled a choice morsel in it, a customary sign of friendship or approval, and gave the sop to Judas. Judas had his second appeal. His feet had been washed with the rest. Now the mark of favour was offered him, but his resolve was hardened now. 'Do quickly what you are going to do', Christ said. Judas rose and went out. 'And it was night.' John's acute visual memory would never forget the horrifying symbol as the door opened and shut on the traitor. That oblong of darkness . . .

Could not anyone recall moments of joy and gladness, shock or shame, round which memory can weave the whole context of sight and sound? John had such a memory strongly developed, and half a century later he recalled every detail. Did Peter too? In his epistle he uses the expression 'gird yourselves' twice. On the first occasion (1:1:13), he uses the word used by John when he describes his friend as pulling his cloak about him and leaping out of the boat on Galilee to be first ashore. On the second occasion, when he bids his flock to 'put humility as a garment', he uses a verb related to the linen towel with which Christ girded himself that night. Accident? Most probably not. One sees much if one reads in Greek. It hold the mind's attention, and sharpens understanding.

Perhaps a pause should be made here. Words of deep and eternal significance were spoken, and then, as though to postpone his arrest for an hour, they left the room and went to the court of the temple. The figure of the vine and branches which opens the resumption of the theme was, one may guess, suggested, in a manner close to Christ's teaching method, by the white marble of the vine over the temple gate, gloriously marked by the black shadows under the Passover moon. Where better to frustrate his pursuers for a time, than to go to the very centre of their power? John remembered every word, no strange phenomenon except to the growing host of those who are slaves to memory aids and mechanical devices to replace the processes of the human brain. The extraordinary power of memory, is not sufficiently known today . . .

Yes, I found it an illuminating experience to read John intensively, and listen to what he actually sought to say. One knows, then, what to think of such critics and purveyors of personal prejudice as Rudolph Bultmann, who, in the words of the veteran archaeologist, W. F. Albright, has carried on 'an unremitting campaign for decades' against our evangelist. There are some controversial discussions in classical studies in which competent scholars differ. For myself I do not think Euripides wrote the little tragedy called 'Rhesus.' Others think he did. Would any of us consider it a cause for 'unremitting campaigning'? Of course not. Why then in the case of the Fourth Gospel? The reason must be sought in a corner of the campaigner's personality. At which we must leave him. We need not linger over Rudolph. There is more to be said of John.

5: Introduction to Higher Criticism

I have been looking again this evening at John A. T. Robinson's scholarly book on the dating of the documents of the New Testament. The author, a few people will still remember, some score of years ago when he was Bishop of Woolwich, sought to popularise the teachings of Paul Tillich in his odd little paperback *Honest to God*, dubbed by some as a confession of atheism, by others of pantheism, and by few as a contribution to Christian thought.

Proceeding from Woolwich to a chaplaincy at Cambridge and, one may perhaps presume, becoming less encumbered in thought about the canons of literary and historical investigation common enough to the world of classical scholarship, but often so lamentably muddled in Biblical studies, John Robinson fell to self-questioning. He began to ask himself, he tells us, just why any of the New Testament books need be dated later than A.D. 70. On this issue at least the late Bishop of Woolwich ended in a position to the right of my own, for I still feel sure that the historical background favours the belief that the Gospel of John, ancient and indeed recorded though some of it may have been, is best placed in the second half of Domitian's principate, nearer the end of the first century.

The sad feature of the small autobiographical touches in Robinson's fine book of 1976, is his failure to begin to ask the right questions until so late in his career. I have always assumed that to begin with the right questions in any quest for truth in literary or historical studies, was the first step towards discovering the correct answers. The next step demands a thorough knowledge of the text and material in view, and a steadfast, honest look at what it claims to be.

How truly regrettable it is that a good scholar should so long postpone the first essentials for any investigation. Robinson's concluding words are as naive as they are tragic: '. . . Dates remain disturbingly fundamental data.' Could anything be more obvious? And one might have thought that the fate of F. C. Bauer and his Tübingen School of New Testament criticism, of more than a century ago, a ludicrous structure of assumption wrecked on a few emerging papyrological and archaeological facts, had finally taught scholars not to begin with convenient, spectacular, or novel theories, and accommodate the requred dates to fit them. If dates are 'disturbing' in any way, they are so only to those whose hasty and vulnerable theories are unprotected against their damaging impact.

I can remember how, in those days of my first preoccupation with the text of the Fourth Gospel, I looked forward to a fuller scrutiny of the relevant literature. My interest was strongly stirred by a book which came my way, *The Living Christ and the Four Gospels,* by R. W. Dale, predecessor of J. H. Jowett at Carr's Lane Congregational Church in my natal city of Birmingham. Published in 1904, it is a tribute to the intelligence of that city congregation, for it is a series of quite demanding lectures on the four evangelists, and made me more vividly aware of a field waiting to be explored, when the heavy demands on me as a University lecturer, should allow me time to expand reading in that area. Meanwhile my knowledge of the content and lower criticism of John, were laying down the proper foundations. Dale's lectures confirmed what I already knew, that the methods of literary investigation applied equally to the New Testament, as they did to other writers of the first century – no great array, I might add, apart from Tacitus, Seneca, Josephus, Pliny.

My opportunity for such wider study came in an unexpected fashion. Odd things happen in one's career which seem at the time catastrophe, but with the passage of the years, and under the wise hand of God, work 'into a pattern for good', as Paul puts it. My chief and mentor, Professor A. C. Paterson, died, over a weekend, just too early for the discovery of the penicillin which would have saved him. It was too early, too, for me to succeed him in the Chair of Classics, a promotion for which he was grooming me. Life was dramatically changed, I thought tragically. My plans for work on the text of Lucretius at Oxford under Cyril Bailey, went by the board. The new incumbent reduced the teaching load in the busy Department catastrophically. There is no other word, but the chaos was not now my responsibility. But that distant story is of no interest here, and I introduce it without even an attempt to draw a moral.

The result, was, however, literally a benediction. My teaching reduced, tutorials suspended, and with academic counselling confined to the head of the Department, I was left with a good deal more than half my working week free for full seven years until, curiously enough, in a rescue operation, the University authorities divided the Department of Classics and gave me sole control of Greek – for seven years, until my appointment to the Chair of Classics.

Grasping with both hands an opportunity never likely, I realised, to come my way again, I set to work to read. A. C. Paterson had left to the University a magnificent library. It was the University's good fortune, for he was about to change that will. I acquired German and Italian. I already had an Honours degree in French, and I went to work systematically on that multitude of books and bound periodicals. I concentrated on the Augustan poets, Greek drama and those other spheres on which much of my teaching and writing were to be based, the interrelation of history and geography for example, the emerging corpus of archaeological literature, and the history of the first century, where Mediterranian history and the New Testament overlap.

Above all I could now turn, properly equipped with the correct discipline, to New Testament criticism. I began with John's Gospel which, as a Greek book, I knew. That dates were 'fundamental data' was to me no news. Theories about composition and authorship necessarily depend on the time of writing. There, and there only one begins. And, tangled with determination of the date and place of composition, is a feeling for a period, a sense of appropriateness, an awareness of atmosphere, which is an instinct acquired, not material to be picked up like the paradigm of a verb. When Sherwin-White, one of the recent classicists to discover the New Testament, speaks of something which could only have been put down by someone who lived at such and such a time, I know what he means.

It was my great surprise, when I first began to read widely among New Testament commentators, to discover that they not only lacked such perception, but, more pitiably still, were quite unaware that they lacked it. I found them prone to commence with a theory, as if it was a theme prescribed by a tutor for a Ph.D. thesis, and a tutor at his wit's end to think of enough subjects for a class too big for him. Indeed, it is quite possible that some of the more extravagant nonsense from German universities in particular had no more responsible origin.

Theories can be notions that brush the surface of the mind. I am not at all averse to allowing the imagination to roam a little. Documented events can be arranged and set in their juxtapositions and relationships in patterns thought to be reasonable. But all such activities should be subject to scrutiny, to the discovery of new fragments of evidence. It is truth which is to be sought, and nothing less than the truth, certainly not a pet hobby horse, a gross prejudice or a scholar's 'reputation', none of which are worth defending at truth's expense.

We left the theme of John's Gospel in the preceding chapter at the point where that exquisite and poignant last teaching, perhaps in the temple precincts, was under examination. But proceed beyond this. Could the tense narrative of the confrontation with Pilate have been written by other than an eye-witness? This, in fact, is the point that should command the closest attention of historians ranging far wider than those who seek to describe and elucidate the Gospel of John. The very tension of the narrative, from the pen of a Galilean fisherman, demands precisely the situation in which it claims to be set. Nowhere else in the few surviving records of the time can a fascinated reader watch a minor Roman governor, compromised by his past, trapped by the junta he had sought to pacify, and fighting for his career, as Pilate was. Add the interlocking details of Matthew's story and Luke's, and the ring of truth is audible. But in John's narrative, closer and confessedly the account of an eyewitness, the effect is startling.

Here was a man in mortal fear. I had studied deeply the eastern frontier policy of the two emperors, Augustus and Tiberius. The north-eastern frontier had less definition, behind its vulnerable Euphrates, than the western provinces found behind that perilously long dividing line of the Rhine and the Danube. Ever imperial improvisers, the Empire's rulers always used any form of local government which could meet their purpose. Procurators, stewards directly responsible to Caesar (hence the availability of Paul's direct 'appeal'), were the choice of Tiberius. But anyone with knowledge of Tiberius, lonely, impatient, a disciplinarian, can read to some extent what went on in Pilate's mind. He could not afford another complaint from the Jews, even an unreasonable complaint. Perhaps Pilate was already a tool of Seianus' ambitions, for the praetorian prefect had at least his later schemes in mind. Nor let anyone underestimate the deep awareness of the Jewish leaders of all the cross-currents of politics in Rome itself. Pilate, of all people, would not trust them not to turn many an interlocking wheel, if they set their minds to it.

A more exact picture of a stupid ruler's dilemma could not be imagined. Here was a man whose one responsibility was to keep a small and vital province on the arc of Rome's most exposed frontier at peace. He knew, when he was appointed to the position, that this involved the correct management of the most intractable people in the world, and of a network of collaborating groups whose covert hostilities and inscrutable motives were enough to baffle the cleverest and most subtle administrators. Pilate was neither clever nor subtle. I had studied Tiberius closely especially in Tacitus' prejudiced account. I could feel the reality of that Jerusalem trial, the obvious disruption of the Jews' plot to corrupt the judge, Pilate, alarmed perhaps by his anxious wife, battling for time and retreating to formality in a manner calculated to exasperate the vicious priests . . .

It passed my understanding how anyone who understood the nature of historiography, let alone knew the time and place, could imagine the faintest trace of 'myth' here. To go through the account phrase by phrase, as well as to absorb its total impact, is to gain precisely the same impression. The savage taunt about 'the King of the Jews' from an infuriated Pilate could only be placed in the historical situation in which it occurs. And who could invent the snapped phrase of three words: 'What I have written, I have written.'

Space and time are needed for the growth of fiction, much less what they call myth, to assume shape and take root. There was no time. That is why a proper respect for the chronological data, and the wider context of history, can emancipate the student from much nonsense. The conclusion that the writer was mistaken, misconceived his facts, distorted them, can still be obstinately held. But let us be spared ludicrous theories which demand writing of a species which cannot be accommodated here. 'What bad writing', said Dean Inge with irritation when he read the Gospels through in Greek during an Aegean cruise. As a matter of fact, in the linguistic and literary context, the three accounts of the trial of Christ were quite distinguished pieces of reporting. The Dean misconceived the whole pattern of events. Matthew's Gospel is just what one would expect, if the tradition is to be accepted that, like Thomas, as we know since 1956, and like Peter, if a fragment of De Joinville the French chronicler, is valid evidence, Matthew collected 'the words of the Lord.' At some later time the interconnecting narrative was added. The Gospel, like its companions, is not an ordered biography. The taxman from Capernaum was not a practised or practising historian. But this does not preclude veracity, and the First Gospel is what one would expect to find given the mode of composition. As well judge the literary capacity of Inge by a handful of sermon notes, with their relevant quotation.

Mark is a rugged little book. It was built out of the material which Peter, Mark's 'father in God', supplied. An attuned ear can catch the sound of Peter's voice. If Peter's letters are to be accepted as authentic, and there are no valid reasons why they should not be so regarded, it is possible to catch the scent of fire in the air, as the climate changed in Rome, and the first five years of Nero's principate began to move towards the grim tragedy of A.D. 69, so vividly detailed in Tacitus. Mark's hasty text is just what one would expect, if Peter, alarmed at the mounting storm, set out in haste to have his 'preaching material' recorded. It is not 'badly written.' If it were a new discovery, like the recent Marcan or pre-Marcan fragment from the Qumran cave, it would be hailed as an astonishingly clear picture of events.

And Luke. It is good, competent Greek, not finally written up, though Luke's opening paragraphs in both his books, suggest that, had he so wished, he could have written in the manner and style of the Greek historians. It is reasonable to assume that Luke did what he set out to do, to collect available data and to process and examine it in the fashion in which a physician in Hippocrates' tradition might be expected to do. The careful opening chapters might indicate that among those he interviewed in those presumed two years of leisure, while Paul was in Rome's protective custody in the garrison port of Caesarea, was the aged Mary. Luke wrote well. His story of the Emmaus road is magnificent. If Zacchaeus' story is syntactically Semitic, what is more likely than that he translated direct from the Jericho taxman's own account. Traces proper to the Gentile writer and to the friend of Paul are discernible to the sensitive reader.

And of John, I have said enough. It is as one would expect an aged eyewitness to write, when there were corners of the Church exposed to crass misunderstanding. It is in good, simple Greek, that Common Dialect which arose from a basic Attic. Since comparative youth I have read two classical languages with something of the ease with which I read my own, and I weary of the linguistic criticisms of those without feeling for a language in its context of time, place and purpose. Any writer or speaker of a modern language other than his own, knows that he is no position to judge style or to catch the finer subtleties of speech until he speaks or at least reads in the alien medium without a faint ghosting of English translation behind the words, and without a consciousness of a language to which he was not born.

To achieve such ease in an ancient language, Latin or Greek, is not a condition easily attained. Perhaps only a professional classicist with daily teaching and study, and long years of necessary concentration on the material of his vocation, can reach such salutary familiarity. I look upon it as one of the greatest treasures of good fortune that life has brought me that the ancient languages, and ancient history were the very material of my livelihood. I could wish that I had such ease in Semitic languages.

But this is why I speak, I claim, with some justified assurance, when I say that the New Testament is not written in a clumsy patois, that it can rise to heights of power, that it is a flexible and potent medium of expression . . . Much less should it be doubted that Galilean Jews such as Peter and John could not have attained the powerful grasp of Greek they both had, when that language had probably been their second speech since childhood with the Decapolis just across the lake, and a long expatriate familiarity with great Greek cities in a mobile world.

In these days when the old disciplines of a classical education are so widely forgotten, it may be difficult to realise that students were once trained to write in the style of Cicero or of Demosthenes, and that competent classicists in senior university classes could make fair attempts at rendering a piece of English into the style of, say, Tacitus or Xenophon. I have routinely set such exercises, and provided model translations in more than one style. There is no finer way of developing a linguistic consciousness. It would be no impossible task for a sound Greek scholar to rewrite, shall we say the first letter of Peter, in the simpler style of the first letter to John. Given a few weeks to pick up some tricks of intonation, accentuation and pronunciation, the same scholar could make his way in Athens or Ephesus.

These remarks are made only to deprecate the paying of too much attention to New Testament scholars who are prone to pontificate on the linguistic standards and style of their authors, without adequately knowing their works within the wider context of the Greek language. There is no intention to discourage the acquisition of even a little Greek, and, indeed, some ability to read the New Testament in its original language should be more common among Christians, whose book of faith the New Testament is. A minimum of Greek can be a valuable instrument of study, a delightful experience of intimacy, and certainly no impossible task, as many have found whom I have persuaded to begin. Greek is not a difficult language, but it is Greek which should rather be learned, not something called 'New Testament Greek'. Even that narrower approach, however, is not without interest and usefulness.

The fact, indeed, I found to be one of the simple pleasures of taking students of what was to be the Bible College of New Zealand, word for word, through the Greek of John's Gospel. They had behind them a year of Greek grammar, one subject of many. It was necessary to analyse phrase by phrase, explaining each form of verb and noun. The response of those classes, filling 40 years, demonstrated to me the pleasure and enlightenment which a very little acquaintance with Greek can give. 'He came to his own things', to give one example, 'and his own people did not take him in.' So John 1:11. Turn the readers to 19:27 and Acts 21:6, and Luke 18:28. The same neuter plural is clear to anyone who can recognise a neuter plural, and obviously the phrase means 'home'. 'He came home and his own folk would not let him in.' How it adds to the poignancy of the incarnation and the rejection of the living Lord. And yet of all the translators, which number over 50, Godspeed alone seems to use the obvious turn of phrase.

Take another neuter plural at John 6:66. Any beginner, picking his way word by word, can see that the words run literally 'many went to the things behind, and no longer kept with him.' And they will realise that, in Phil. 3:13 Paul has a vivid word to say of 'the things behind.' It is exactly the same phrase. 'The things behind', to which some less valiant souls returned, were not necessarily reprehensible modes of life. Most of them, except Matthew, could have returned without reproach to their old life. But how much more apparent the situation is when the literal rendering of the Greek fastens attention upon it. Nor does it require more than the simple parsing of a verb to observe that the words translated 'should not perish' in 3:16, are the same words, voice, mood, tense and all, as those rendered in 6:12 'that nothing be wasted'. Why not, then, transpose and make a striking translation? '. . . that whosoever believes in him should not be wasted . . .' Incidentally, anyone with the rudiments of grammar can see that the verb in question is one of those forms which is both passive, and what Greek grammar calls 'middle'. Grammar is a pattern imposed upon a given mass of linguistic phenomena. Strictly there is no difference between middle and passive. The middle is a form of the verb in which the subject is deeply involved in the act implied by the verb. It becomes necessary to make parsing decisions, only when the necessities of translation into a language which has no conveniently parallel devices to render the full meaning, demand it. Thus the word 'perish' of the famous verse (a good rendering) does not mean literally and completely 'should not be destroyed' (passive), or 'should not destroy himself' (middle). It means both, and a neat three-point sermon emerges: 'be wasted', 'be destroyed', 'destroy himself.' All are true, and illustrate the difficulty of translating any one language into another. The reader of Greek who knows the language intimately, has no difficulties in such semantic contexts. He simple apprehends the verb in its entirety.

63

There are several contexts in which a beginner, plodding through the text is alerted to a fuller meaning. The unfortunate KJV rendering of John 2:4 becomes immediately clear. The vigour returns, emancipated from familiar and stately English, to such conversations as that by the Sychar well, and the discussion about the blind man, and that man himself before the Pharisees, where word echoes and word order sometimes carry their own message. We have already looked at this. Consider such minutiae as prepositional prefixes. Looking more closely at the story of the beach on Galilee in John 21, I noticed recently a small detail. It might be of interest to mention first in passing a sentence which had turned me to the passage in the evangelist's last chapter. 'Are these resurrection stories true?' wrote a leading churchman, supplying a brief introduction to a modern translation of John. No, of course not, was his bland reply. They are lovely symbols. The net was the Church, and, since 'the ancients' believed that the fish of the seas fell into 153 species, the writer, an ecumenical personality ahead of his times, hoped that the undivided Church would hold all nations.

I had thought that such imaginings, not unlike Loisy on the then undiscovered Bethesda Pool, had gone out of favour most of half a century ago, but the figure for 'the ancients'' belief was attributed to Ossian, a little known poet who left us some 600 lines on fish and fishing, and was quoted, I discovered, by St. Jerome in a commentary on Ezekiel. (Aristotle and Pliny both gave another figure, but no matter). The first instinct of a sound literary critic would surely be to examine his authorities. Did the boring Ossian, in the second century or the fourth, in Cilicia or Syria (so little we know), actually allege this? I was saved much work of investigation by the tireless editor of Ossian in the Loeb Edition. I assure you that, if you include sponges and crustaceans as fish, you can just reach 152, and that is all, and always will be. Nor will the texts allow John to be reduced to the lower figure. It would be pathetic were not such outrageous statements not dangerous to trusting readers.

But it was while I was looking again at the text that I saw that 21:11 says: 'Peter went up and dragged the net to the shore.' Now Peter was in the midst of an unrecorded conversation with Christ. He had leaped into the water and splashed ashore to be sure of the opportunity to speak thus alone. He sees the overburdened net being dragged into the stony beach – his net. And how typical of the earthly, downright man Peter is always shown to be, that he interrupts the spiritual for the practical and hurries to the rescue, of John, too, who, typical of a fisherman, and also of one uncommonly preoccupied with numbers, that he should count the fish. But 'Peter went up.' Why the preposition? Either he climbed aboard again, and the word is not rare in the sense of embarking, or 'he waded out', for verbs containing 'up' are standard Greek for pushing off from the shore, just as their opposites, prefixed with 'down', are standard terms for putting into shore. I prefer 'waded out'. The usage, of course, is based on the illusion of water rising from the beach. The Greeks knew, as well as we do, that a ship did not 'sail up' to the horizon, but it can look that way. But observe how this tiny detail, so visible in the Greek (though no translation has adopted it) touches the whole picture of events with reality and humanity. The critics are naive, as C. S. Lewis put it in an essay on this theme. Lewis was a classicist, an English scholar, a linguist and a trained literary critic. He is a little impatient with Bultmann and his obedient tribe. 'These men ask me to believe they can read between the lines of the old texts, the evidence is their obvious inability to read (in any sense worth discussing) the lines themselves. They claim to see fern-seed and can't see an elephant ten yards away in broad daylight.' Therein lies my point. Even stumbling through the Greek text does force one to read the lines and look at what is said. And if the word about fern-seed puzzles you see Shakespeare (Henry IV 1, 2.1.95). I continue to campaign for more learning of Greek among Christians, though I do deprecate the quoting of 'the Greek' until some solid progress has been made.

Allow another touch of illumination from the preposition

unobtrusively embedded in a verb. The passage about the woman 'taken in adultery', in John 8, happens to be one on which the texts are divided. The Lower Criticism, as with the verse about the angel at the Bethesda Pool, presents an equally divided case from the most ancient manuscripts. But, unlike the situation in John 5, the Higher Criticism is decisively in favour of the retention of the story. It is so like Christ, so true to the whole position in time and place, so ringing with authenticity. Ascetic copyists suppressed it. John included it.

No linguistic analysis in such a short and constricted sample can say that this is not John's style and language. Always be suspicious of dogmatism on 'style'. As in the case of any other form of art, it is a matter of supreme delicacy and difficulty to identify individual characteristics in language, unless the material at hand is abundant. But observe how Christ 'looks up', literally 'bends up' or straightens himself from that writing in the dust. He had a way of looking down when he was weary with pettiness, hatred, quibbling priests and the like, one of the few personal details recorded of him apart from his spoken words. Look at Luke's story of the widow at the treasury: 'Looking up' he saw the visitors making their contributions. He had been sitting with eyes cast down. The bullying, sneering questioners had briefly left him, hurrying no doubt to some religious exercise. He was tired to exhaustion by it all. Then suddenly arousing, he 'looked up'. We seem to catch an intimate glimpse of the Lord.

But let us pause for a moment, perhaps halfway through this book, and ask what we are achieving. This is not a commentary on the Fourth Gospel. That is a task I have yet to undertake, if time allows, and someone shows desire for it. John's story of Christ has been almost a theme in this and the preceding chapter, but that was because his tormented Gospel was my introduction to the study of modern New Testament criticism, and the mighty disillusionment with its methods and standards which it provoked in me.

I began my New Testament studies with the *Expositor's*

Greek Testament, whose five volumes were given me by the man who provoked my committment to Christ. I spent some twelve months on the task, and branched out from them into the 'authorities' and fields of study, the ancient evidence, and the themes of investigation thus suggested. I discovered that conservative scholarship was rising to its feet, that the liberals had not complete control, but that there was wide need for more men and women, especially for those adequately trained in ancient history and classical literature, to turn attention to the New Testament.

Since those days 30 and 40 years ago, much, enormously much, has been done. Archaeology, here as in other parts of the Bible, has had much to say. The nomenclature and geography of the Gospel has been established. You can count the 'porches' in the Bethesda Pool, and stand upon 'the Pavement', scored and scratched by the markings of the soldiers' games. You can look at the immense stone lying broken where the Tenth Legion's battering rams pushed it, amid the extramural fragments of the Old City. You can read its inscription: 'Place of the Trumpet', and guess what the evil Caiaphas meant when he feared the Romans would 'take away our place and nation' . . . and a dozen other details.

This is the story of a personal encounter. I shall pass on to others of like nature, but, if there is a book with which I have lived intimately for a lifetime, it is the account of his Master written by the aged Bishop of Ephesus, John the son of Zebedee. He holds me as convinced today that he was telling the truth, as I was when I first looked closely into his pages of simple Greek. I am still held by his affidavit that the told the truth, that he did hear a soldier call a spear a 'hyssos', that he deliberately omitted details of what happened when he was taking Mary home, as he was bidden to do, that he did see the water from the damaged lungs mingle with the blood, and saw 'the linen clothes lying and the cloth that had been about his head folded into itself apart . . .' That revealing prepositional prefix again. How authentic it is.

6: Discovering Luke and Paul

Joseph Kemp, of Auckland's Baptist Tabernacle, the man under whose sturdy preaching I found Christ in 1921, died of a brain tumour in 1933. I acquired a considerable number of books from his large library. That is how I made my first acquaintance with the fine theological writings of James Denney and the magnificent 'apologetic' works (I never quite like that adjective) of James Orr. The contributions of both stalwarts to conservative Christian thinking came in the closing years of the nineteenth century and the early days of our own. I wish they had come my way in the twenties, when I could have done with their strength and sanity. On the other hand, in that toilsome decade I was heavily engaged in putting down the bases of my professional classical scholarship, and there is no doubt that the simultaneous and intense preoccupation with the textual criticism of the New Testament and especially of John's Gospel which I have already described, was part of God's rough-hewing of my life.

But along with Orr and Denney came their contemporary, William Mitchell Ramsay, a complete set of whose works in their first editions came to me from Kemp's library. And coming in 1934 this major acquisition of scholarship coincided with the undemanding years in the Classics Department which I was using to such advantage. Ramsay, I at once recognised, was my man, not a professional theologian but a fellow classicist, who held chairs of classical studies, art, archaeology and Latin diversely, in Oxford and Aberdeen, into my own lifetime. It was the catastrophe of 1914 which terminated his 24 years of research into the antiquities of Western Asia Minor, but not before he had pioneered the study of classical archaeology, a decade before the first volumes of the *Cambridge Ancient History* laid the foundations of the vast and continuing contribution of that developing science to all investigation of the past. This was already part of my awareness, and it was a relief and a delight to find the apocalyptic obscurities of the Book of Revelation acquiring their proper significance in the literature of the first century, under the skilful treatment Ramsay brought to the material remains and records of the past. I did not need to be made aware of a line of study which I have majored upon in both Classics and the Bible, the interweaving of geography and history. Along with archaeology, Ramsay always stressed the supreme relevance of geography. He also made me a little wistfully conscious of the need to see personally significant localities, however efficiently geography fulfils the function its name implies. I did not forsee how rich my own experience of travel in such quests was to be. Ramsay did not leave us until the sombre days of 1939, and I have regretted that I did not give an old man (he was 88) the pleasure of a note of appreciation on what he had meant to me.

It was his books *The Church in the Roman Empire*, and *Paul the Traveller and Roman Citizen*, of 1893 and 1895 respectively, which launched me on a lifelong interest in the early decades of the Church, and brought me into contact with Luke, a Greek historian of standing in his own right, and with the massive mind of Paul, 'the first European,' the man who first wove into one in his own person the three cultures which engendered the West, a privilege which every Christian classicist shares with peculiar pleasure.

Ramsay's discovery of Luke was much more dramatic than mine. Ramsay had before him a traditional classical career. The staple of scholarship at Oxford and Cambridge was Classics, the literature, thought and history of Greece and Rome. In both, Ramsay achieved academic distinction. He was a Fellow successively of Exeter and Lincoln Colleges, after which (in 1886) he took the chair of Humanity (or Latin) at Aberdeen. It was before, during, and after this tenancy, that he undertook the archaeological and epigraphical researches in the rich and almost untouched field of the old Roman province of Asia, and the central cities of the peninsula, which was to be his enormous contribution to Biblical studies.

Ramsay had no solid Christian faith, beyond a sincere hunger for truth and God. In the over-trustful manner of some classicists, who assume too readily that the critical methods of the Biblical scholars are as austere as their own, he accepted the commonly radical conclusions of German scholarship. F. C. Bauer, initiator of the so-called Tübingen School, died in 1860, when Ramsay was a boy of nine years, but the ideas of that sceptically turbulent era were widely abroad and when Ramsay, financed by some research grant, set out for Asia Minor, it was assumed that Luke was a spurious second century piece of writing and of course not in any way reliable for first century investigations. This was all 'assured conclusions' – 'sicherlich' was a word such critics found it difficult to do without. Ramsay had no intention of spending time on the discredited records of the New Testament. But Ramsay had an honest mind, a necessary possession for anyone who has a zeal for truth. Reappraisement can indeed be agonising. It is unpleasant to throw treasured lecture notes into the basket, but few true scholars have never had to face that necessity. That is why Ramsay saw only one conclusion when local inscriptions, evidence more solid than the geographers' speculations, established the fact that when, as recorded in Acts 14:6, 'they fled into Lystra and Derbe, cities of Lycaonia', Paul and Barnabas did cross an administrative border-line. Luke was right. The frontier of Lycaonia lay where he said it did. It was a turning point in Ramsay's studies.

It might be interesting to quote his actual words, written in 1898. 'I may fairly claim to have entered on this investigation without prejudice in favour of the conclusion I shall now seek to justify . . . I began with a mind unfavourable to it, for the ingenuity and apparent completeness of the Tübingen theory had at one time quite convinced me. It did not then lie in my line of life to investigate the subject minutely, but more recently I found myself brought in contact with the Book of Acts as an authority for the topography, antiquities and society of Asia Minor. It was gradually borne in upon me that in various details the narrative showed marvellous truth . . . I came to find it a useful ally in some obscure and difficult investigations . . .' Bauer is actually on record for calling statements in Acts 'intentional deviations from historical truth.'

It is quite tragic how eminent classicists have trusted that quite different school, the Biblical scholars, as colleagues concerned with the same canons of investigation, or, more tragically, have not recognised the documents of the New Testament, as a collection of detailed writings, germane, and indeed belonging to their own field of studies. The prejudice, understandable in the light of what some New Testament writers have stated, continued long after a more salutary awareness should have emerged. *The Oxford Classical Dictionary*, for example, first appeared in 1949. Its article on Tarsus, a mere 180 words, from the major authority on the eastern cities of the Empire, Professor A. H. M. Jones, mentions in closing that during the first century B.C., Tarsus was the seat of a celebrated philosophical school. Ramsay, in his *Cities of Saint Paul* (1907), has 150 pages on the city. I wrote to the editor and suggested that a second edition might allow 200 words in order that it might be added that Tarsus' chief claim to fame was that it was the birthplace of Paul, perhaps at or just after the beginning of the century in question, Paul the converted rabbi whose writings changed the course of history. They did, and a trifle meagrely, Jones complied.

The New Testament is, in Acts and Paul's letters, an intimate and vivid authority on life in the ancient and renowned city of Corinth. P. N. Ore, no mean historian, contributes a column and a half to Corinth, does not list Luke and Paul among the ancient authorities, and manages to limit the Christian historical involvement in the theme to one word. Corinth was 'visited by apostles, emperors, philosophers and earthquakes.'

It is a situation which is by way of changing. For example, in A. N. Sherwin-White's book of some 20 years ago on Roman law and society in the New Testament, Ramsay's judgment is repeated and reinforced by an eminent classicist and historian, who betrays no personal regard for the New Testament as 'a sacred text' whatsoever. Proper to his purpose as an historian, he deplores the neglect of a large corpus of evidence. He stresses the exactitude especially of Luke's historical framework, the precision of time and place, the feel and tone of city-life in the Greco-Roman world, seen through the eyes of a supremely intelligent Hellenistic Jew. Luke, he says, 'takes us on a conducted tour of the Greek and Roman world with detail and narrative so interwoven as to be inseparable.' The book embodies his Sarum Lectures of 1960, 1961.

Nor does Sherwin-White hide his astonishment at the work of the New Testament scholars who so readily sold the pass, especially the 'form critics' and their gloomy conclusion that 'the historical Christ is unknowable and the history of his mission cannot be written.' Drily he adds that classical historians profess to hold a fairly clear idea about the person and policies of 'Christ's best-known contemporary,' Tiberius Caesar, for all that the chief source for Tiberius is the historian Tacitus, who hated Tiberius for introducing the practice of the common informer which Domitian used so savagely against his senatorial enemies in the time of Tacitus, who wrote some 70 years after Tiberius had gone. It is pleasant sometimes in the academic world to see a surge of scholarship flow in the direction in which one has sought to drive one's craft against contrary currents for years enough.

It was good to follow Ramsay through his new-found discoveries, Luke's exactitude in the use of the correct geographical and administrative terms with wealthy evidence derived from epigraphical and payrological discoveries. It was also, I vividly recall, round those years before the First War, and in the twenties which at last permitted life and scholarship to resume, that Moulton and Milligan and other papyrologists were flooding the world of New

Testament studies with evidence from Egypt which gave life and background to the book. The understanding of the language of the New Testament which began with J. H. Moulton's *Prolegomena* in 1907, was still flowing with Nigel Turner's third volume in 1963, and there is annually more to say. It was exciting to watch it all grow from Adolf Deissmann's heavy-handed use of the papyri to the evaluations of later scholarship, and at a time when I was at leisure to read, think and watch.

But this drifts from the chapter's theme. The words I wrote concluding the last paragraph brought me back to it – my discovery of Luke as an historian through William Mitchell Ramsay. He sharpened my principles of historical research with his remarkable smaller book, *Was Christ Born at Bethlehem?* Ramsay was challenged to apply his confident use of Lucan documents to the miraculous story of the Nativity. Of course, the ultimate judgment must be in the last analysis depend upon the veracity of the most famous and revered woman of all time, Mary, mother of Christ. So, indeed, does much of what is set down generally as history. In writing autobiographically in several different contexts in the last few years, I am constantly made aware of how much depends upon my own unsupported word. It conveys a deep responsibility.

Luke, nevertheless, had a trained mind. In his medical studies and practice, he must have been in the Hippocratic tradition, and the Greeks over many centuries led the world in their understanding of the processes of human thought. In the opening of his Gospel, he gives solemn assurance that he has properly and honestly looked into the facts. The dates suggest that he had the two years of Paul's sequestration in the garrison town of Caesarea to range the little land, no bigger than Wales, where survivors of Christ's day lived in large numbers. Among them, as the splendid intimacy of Luke's opening chapters suggests, could have been Mary. Or, if the tradition is entertained that the Virgin moved to Ephesus, that was a city Luke knew well enough. Assurances such as Luke gives, like oaths, were taken more seriously in the ancient world than they are sometimes taken today, and it is not naive to assume that Luke looked carefully into the story of the Nativity and the Annunciation, and found no cause for dismissing Christ's mother as a liar. He certainly had no cause to deceive.

It is therefore reasonable to begin with such an author's affidavit, until he is convicted of deliberate falsehood or culpable credulity, neither of which charges can be levelled at Luke. It is then proper to continue with as close a scrutiny of the personalities involved as the evidence permits. They pass muster as people, and indeed suffered, died, and gained no material advantage, human fashion, by maintaining their claim to veracity. It is then a sound procedure to set the whole complex of events and circumstances in the context of time, place and society, and to examine the whole for incongruities or distortions of the sort which an alert historical mind can discern or sense.

From this the historian proceeds, as Ramsay did, to test his confirmed confidence in Luke in the area of Luke's most astonishing statements. There are circumstances capable of historical evaluation and confirmation. How came it about, that Joseph and Mary, who appear to have been from the town of Nazareth at the other end of the land, were in the ancient town of Bethlehem, at a time which was inconvenient for an expectant mother, if not positively perilous? Ramsay set to work on the papyrological evidence for the periodic Roman census. He found a public notice of a bare century later, directing the population to assemble in their family or natal territory on a certain date. The Governor of Egypt, who signed this particular document, recognises the strain upon accommodation and food supplies, and is in the act of announcing emergency arrangements when the document, becomes too worn and tattered to read. It is exactly the situation of the 'crowded inn'. Ramsay also unearthed actual census documents going back to A.D. 48. In a word he pressed specific and exact historical examination hard up against the core events, and proved that whatever could be submitted to such investigation stood the test, and sounded a true ring of verity.

I have quoted the documents elsewhere in what I have

had occasion to write, and have also by what seems to me a careful and honest analysis of events, placed the date with some claim to likelihood, in the autumn of 5 B.C. But this is not, as I must repeat, an examination of Luke. It is a chapter on how I discovered the worth of Luke and found Ramsay's acceptance and treatment of the challenge of the Nativity story an elegant piece of historical reasoning of the sort that appeals to the academic mind.

I think I have never enjoyed a year's course of lectures more than those I gave several times, not under Christian auspices, but in my own Department of Classics in the last decade of my activity there. Largely under the promotion of two of my senior assistants Drs B. F. Harris and H. R. Minn, a sub-department of Biblical History and Literature was established. It called for a purely secular approach. We were under obligation not to stress a Christian or a 'religious' aspect of the subject at all. It was thus that I lectured on Acts as a document of first century and classical literature, not at all a difficult task, for so I had trained myself, in the proper contexts, to regard it. But those courses, especially those covering the second half of the book, 'the acts of Paul' as we may call it, apart from 'the acts of Peter', were a delight.

It was fascinating to analyse the strata of that cosmopolitan society which was so well and so painfully reflected in the congregation. Ramsay made an important contribution to historical studies generally when he demonstrated, in the case of the apocalyptic letters to seven of the hundreds of churches of the Province of Asia, that the spirit of a populace, shaped out of the locality and history of their general community, expressed itself in the collective personality of the indigenous Christian group. In no centre was this illuminating theory better demonstrated than in the ancient town on the Corinth Isthmus. It was rent by the old Greek vice of faction, marred by the exotic cults and vices of a multilingual city, a roaring, turbulent crossroads of Middle Mediterranean trade . . . Or Athens, living on her past greatness, sophisticated, talkative, intellectual, a resort of scholars and the charlatans which haunt such places. To see Paul adapt to Socratic method, to face the most learned legal institution in the world, the Areopagus, and move as easily in the realm of Stoic philosophy as he had moved in the marketplace as a visiting sophist, and at Ephesus as a teaching rabbi, was to feel renewed one's amazement that classical historians should not have all along felt for this authentic glimpse of life in one of history's greatest cities in a century of decline.

In preparing the third Rendle Short Memorial Lecture, which I gave at the University of Bristol in June 1964, I looked closely into the Areopagus Address which was my theme for the occasion, sought to set it in its context of history, society and Pauline evangelism. I look back on that span of reading as another remarkable contact with the great man and his historian. Every phrase in that tiny précis rings true. Paul knew his Stoicism, after all a product of his birthplace. Any sensitive and educated Athenian ear would catch five echoes of surviving literature. The record is a gem of precision, and compact reporting – and yet I am certain that only one who knew Athens, and all Athens had been, could savour with all its sharpness the famous address.

And Ephesus, with all the 'feel' of a great Asian religious centre, with the 'town clerk' in an agony of apprehension over the peril in which the 'free city' stood if the Roman authorities should take an austere view of the 'tumult', as the Romans called such exhibitions of indiscipline. Those supremely sane administrators were ready to allow a multitude of local forms of government to function, from Herodian kingdoms to provincial muncipalities, so long as they 'delivered the goods', that is law and order and steady tribute. In fact we can pick up the people of Ephesus at three different points – the superbly told story of the riot in Acts 19, on which the classical historian, Charles Seltman wrote an essay, Seltman who had no sympathy with Paul, but saw the significance of the account, secondly the congregation, sensed, though not as clearly as the Corinth church, behind Paul's letter, and thirdly John's apocalyptic letter.

Observe details. Although my class on those lecture occasions at the University were working from translations, I myself lectured from the Greek text. I have earlier remarked that the original sharpens observation for detail. The one letter which marks a plural, where one would have expected a singular ('s' in English), is as obvious in the translations as it is in Luke's own story, but there it somehow more sharply strikes the eye. The city official, fighting to quieten the chanting demonstrators, said that no real charges had been laid, there had been no legal enquiry, there was legitimate opportunity for the initiation of such processes, and in the final issue, if all modes of redress and justice should be frustrated, 'there are proconsuls'.

Ephesus was indeed the proconsular seat for the province of Asia, but in no senatorical province was there ever more than one proconsul. Why the plural? It has that sure touch of a vividly remembered phrase. But consider: The vicious Agrippina, one of the evil women of antiquity, had secured her son Nero's accession. A little later, in fact in the autumn of A.D. 54, she was in the consequential process of clearing possible rivals for the principate away. Two imperial stewards were sent to Asia to murder Marcus Junius Silanus, who happened to be the great-grandson of Augustus and a potential danger to Nero in the sinister woman's view. Pending a replacement by the cowed Senate, the two envoys were running the affairs of the province. How completely true to the obsequious attitude of the timid town-clerk, to dignify the two stewards, whose favourable report was vital to the status of Ephesus, with a fictitious official title.

It made me remember the plural 'poets' in the address to the Areopagus in Athens. It was, it appears, two Stoic poets who used the phrase he quoted – and Paul pointedly, a policy he repeated before the Sanhedrin years later, was addressing only a portion of the audience from whom he was likely to win an attentive hearing and a foundation for serious thought. He was a master at reading the minds of his audience, as he demonstrated with the excitable Celtic proletariat at Lystra with his excursion into natural theology.

Did he, on that occasion, find out why the people at the little back-country town set out to worship him? I remember translating to my class the brilliant story from Ovid written half a century before, recounting the legend which made the priest imagine that a Second Coming had taken place. Did Paul find out about the legend? The 'wood, hay and stubble' and 'the gold and silver and precious stones' will make a convincing argument for anyone who cares to read Ovid's welltold tale. And this is not the place to retell what I have told before. My translation and commentary on Luke's book, arose from those lectures in our small department of 'Biblical history and literature'.

So in like fashion have many books I have written. Whether other teachers and writers have observed the phenomenon I do not know, but I have often noticed a certain mental stimulus in speaking about a theme which commands one's confidence and enthusiasm, to a responsive and intelligent group of students. Luke held my attention as he did Ramsay's, and I found, in the way I mention, the flashes of insight, sudden new correlations of this theme and that, rapid cross-referencing between fields of study and an urge to put it all into writing.

I remember how my book on the characters of Euripides arose from a series of lectures I gave on Euripides' last play *The Bacchae*. A series of talks I gave right through one year to a particularly appreciative group at the Bible College of New Zealand, led to my translation and commentary on the first letter of Peter. I had read with particularly close attention the events so luridly described by Tacitus in those years when the 'quinquennium Neronis' – 'Nero's five years', were over. That period of good sane government was the work of Sextus Afranius Burrus, who had been prefect of the praetorian guard Rome's city garrison, since A.D. 51, and Lucius Annaeus Seneca, who was Nero's tutor, who retired after Burrus died in A.D. 62, and was driven to suicide in the context of the bungled conspiracy of Gaius Calpurnius Piso in A.D. 65. When Nero murdered his mother in A.D. 59, a sinister turn of events was clear to every 'Rome-watcher'. Paul reached Rome, perhaps early in A.D. 61, and, in the comparative freedom of his 'hired house', with continued contact with the guards assigned from the praetorians, was on the spot to learn, observe and report, over the vital years of comparative calm before the storm of civil war. That disaster came at the end of the decade when, in 'the year of the four emperors', A.D. 69, 'the Beast was wounded to death and recovered of his deadly wound'. But in the early sixties, there was tremendous activity in the Church to record their vital teachings. The Christian communities had infiltrated Mediterranean society, and the practice of letter-writing, too widely neglected in historical studies, bound the Church together. It is surprising that in general, classical historians have not seen how fitting to the atmosphere of those tense years between A.D. 60 and A.D. 65, Peter's first letter is, even to a clear warning about 'the fiery trial', which was to follow the literal conflagration which engulfed Rome in July A.D. 64, and to the covert warning not to get involved in the conspiracies, which were to culminate in Piso's abortive coup in A.D. 65. Bonhoeffer-fashion they could very well have been tempted to do so. I came to that year's lecturing on Peter from some intensive study in the *Annals* of Tacitus on the climactic years of Nero, and the dreadful story, in that same author's magnificent Latin, of the grim year of quadrilateral civil war, and the explosion of the first rebellion of the Jews. I added, of course, all I could find of consequential literature. I had the deep instinctive feeling which Sherwin-White expresses in his comments on the contemporary relevance of Luke that it was only in the last years before the storm burst on the Roman Christian community in the autumn of A.D. 64, that First Peter could have been written. It was a singular demonstration to me of that interweaving of classical and New Testament studies, and the relevance of each to each, which has formed such a major feature of my academic life, and which, if I should by chance be credited with any contribution to New Testament studies at all, will be seen as what I have sought most consistently to offer.

Many years before I wrote the translation and commentary on Peter's letter, I produced a similar small book on the letter of Paul to Philippi, likewise the byproduct of a course to students, this time a group of Intervarsity Fellowship folk with a zeal (so strong in those days) for solid study. I found the atmosphere of a Roman 'colonia' strikingly convincing. 'Christ is becoming known throughout the whole praetorian barracks', said Paul. It is sad to think that, at the end of that decade, when the German legions ravaged Rome, the praetorians were massacred in the streets – no doubt many among them who had guarded and talked with the notable detainee from Judaea.

To study the last eight chapters of Luke, is to find a wealth of information on the breakdown of Roman rule in Judaea, the mounting pressure which neither priests nor procurators could contain, and the difficulties encountered by local magistrates inadequately equipped with military power or prestige to hold the peace in a situation which drew not a little of its serious peril from the consciousness of international Jewry that in Rome itself matters were reaching crisis proportions. The network of cooperation in the body of international Jewry, which was to be so perilously evident in the second revolt of Hadrian's day, may be seen in much of the story of Paul's last disastrous intrusion into the preserves of metropolitan Jewry. As for law and order, the rescue of Paul by a swift riot squad from the Antonia Fort, is a flash of light on the Judaean situation fascinating for historians. And when one looks at the size of the escort detachment to convey one prisoner down the road to Caesaea, it is to get a glimpse of the collapse of control in a guerrilla-haunted countryside and to wonder, not why the resistance movement erupted, but why it was delayed for another six or seven years before the flash-point came.

The two court scenes, and the demonstration of an appeal to Caesar in action, are as unique. In the vivid story of the wreck of the Alexandrian grainship one can almost taste the salt in the windwhipped air. It was the 'meltemi', the wind sucked out of the snowy European steppes by the hot Sahara, and twirled into a typhoon by the chilly uplands which fill the western end of Crete. 'Badly written', indeed. One almost wonders at first whether Inge knew enough Greek to apprehend style. His academic record, however, in England's Eton-Cambridge context, is unimpeachable, leaving his linguistic blindspot without explanation. As a storyteller, from the tale of Emmaus to the Malta beach, Luke's work is remarkable. As a painter of personality, from the prodigal son to Paul of Tarsus, Luke must be ranked among the best. One cannot know Luke without knowing Luke's near friend. He is one of those in the history of literature, whom a great friendship brought to the knowledge of men. Atticus is known from Cicero, Boswell from Johnson, a dozen Galileans through their fellowship with Christ. I sometimes remember a mossy grave behind a New Plymouth church, where a Taranaki pioneer, Armitage Brown, is buried. His tombstone simply bears the inscription 'the Friend of Keats' . . .

Paul, I have described already as 'the first European.' He was more. Gilbert Murray, who was not a Christian, says he 'was certainly one of the great figures of Greek literature.' And to return, in concluding this chapter, to another classicist, Terrot Reavely Glover might be quoted. I find a small affinity with T. R. Glover. He was a classical historian, who refused to segregate emerging Christianity from its environment. He was once President of the Baptist Union. He was Public Orator of his University. It distantly parallels my own preoccupations and offices. On Paul, Glover says: 'whether one judge the great writers by the number of their readers age after age, or of those whose minds they shape and whose lives they guide, whether we measure them by their gift of transcending their disciples and commentators, and suggesting perpetually new avenues of thought and experience to be explored, or whether we apply to them the test of not merely knowing what to say but how to say it, Paul stands among the greatest of the Greeks . . . who, apart from Homer and Plato, has had so wide and so long an influence, who has opened up so much of the real world to men, whose words have lived more in the hearts of readers?' For myself, I should rank Plato well below, Homer, apart from his influence on Alexander of Macedon, very far below.

With which, if this book is to justify its title, we must leave Luke and Paul . . .

7: Living with the Psalms

Ten happy years after my retirement from the Chair of Classics, were spent as President of the Bible College of New Zealand, the onetime Bible Training Institute founded by my 'father-in-God', Joseph W. Kemp, and in which I taught the Greek John's Gospel from 1927 onward. Today, and I speak from fairly wide acquaintance with such theological teaching establishments, the Bible College of New Zealand is a fine school, impeccably conservative, second to none in the standards of its scholarship, and, after 60 years, remaining a dominant influence in the church of New Zealand.

I succeeded in the presidential chair my old friend Robert Laidlaw of whose influence in my early Christian life I have written eslewhere, and who, as an able business-man, had made an immense contribution to the growth of the College. My own contribution, I knew, would be different. I could not think of my role as simply chairing the meetings of the governing body, and signing graduation certificates. But, as an academic, I did know students, their difficulties, and the world which they would be called upon to meet, its clamour and its criticism. Hence my invention of the 'President's Hour' on Thursday mornings, which I envisaged as an unbriefed and informal talk on any questions which any member of the student body cared to raise, theological, social, academic, anything at all on which I was in a position to speak.

At the same time, it was not possible to fill in a full hour a week answering questions left on slips of paper on the lectern, or sent me by post or telephone during the preceding week. We needed a coherent background, and I chose the Psalms to provide it. For eight years of my decade in the presidency, we went through the Psalms phrase by phrase, word by word. I commonly spent each Sunday afternoon preparing in rough outline what I has to say, and in reading round the theme. That was when I discovered, in the *Expositor's Bible,* the devotional commentary on the Psalms by Alexander Maclaren, whose career as 'the prince of expository preachers' at Union Chapel in Manchester ended in 1903. He died in 1910.

Those were blessed years of understanding and discovery. As a mature Christian I knew the Psalms, but the weekly task of perparation and study I imposed upon myself during these years was akin to that experience with John's Gospel which I have already described. I could wish that I had been able to pursue this course with the linguistic intimacy which, as a professional classicist, I had with Greek. Enough Hebrew, however, to pursue a key word, or an intriguing metaphor through the lexicon, and to uncover parallels and illuminating contexts did show me again what I have mentioned before – the wealth that lies in a basic knowledge of the writer's own language however meagre it may be.

I used very much the varied versions, and found it disappointing that Zondervan's collation of 26 translations of the poetic books of the Old Testament, in which I played a part, seemed so little known. The book revealingly collected significant variations, phrase by phrase, of about half the translations available in English. I found my own assignment, the collation of the Book of Job, one of the most arduous, but rewarding literary tasks I have ever been called upon to undertake.

The variety of achievement in the King James Psalter appears to show that the translators divided that book between several of them of varied capacity. (And, by the way, is it not strange that those who with such confidence similarly distinguish the varied contributors, and redactors of the Old Testament should never have tried to distinguish between the KJV translators? I think one can spot the classical scholarship of the translators of **Peter and Hebrews**, the timidity of the translator of the second letter to Corinth, the bondage to Latin and the Vulgate in some with less Greek – but who would dogmatise? And this is by the way). The translators of the Psalms certainly vary in their touch. Psalm 23 (an exact rendering) is a gem of English literature, and should be protected from all tampering. One could add others.

But observe the stodginess of Psalm 4:1 '. . . thou hast enlarged me when I was in distress'. 'In narrow places you have made space for me', said George Adam Smith, reading into David's evening prayer the imagery of the Judaean wilderness, which, as the Land's great geographer, he knew so well. 'O God my champion', wrote Moffatt, 'when I was hemmed in you have freed me often'. Of course the Hebrew says literally 'enlarged', but need a translator be tied like a third-former poring over his Latin, to literalism of such a sort?

But small discoveries of felicitous renderings were the joy of those eight years. To study thus a corpus of supreme writing, is, as I have more than once discovered in ancient literature at large, to meet not only its authors, but one's remoter predecessors in the field of investigation. One can see the minds of both writers and their editors at work when, in the case of such books as Psalms and Proverbs, collected literature is to be set in a coherent order and arranged in a planned pattern.

In no part of the Bible are we in closer touch with humanity. The Psalter is a book of prayers rather than a prayer book for the second temple, for it must have partially served for the first. Its words spring on to the page hot from the heart of man, torn sometimes by the pain of living, or jubilant at times with joy, in despair or in aspiration, often in outspoken doubt, desolation or self-loathing, but always reaching out for God. That is why the Psalms came to be, and are increasingly through life, a voice for experience, words which seem to understand us, and provide a language for hours of contrition, depression, defeat and triumph. We have the immense advantage of knowing well many of the contributors, most notably the royal poet, David.

I soon became aware, as I spoke weekly on the Psalms and tried to make them relevent to the experience of 200 students, of the patterns which lay in the book. One sees the rabbis' minds at work, particularly, I think, one diligent man, and can observe how the poems were grouped. Sometimes in anonymous writing, it was an informed guess at common authorship, sometimes a visible correspondence in imagery, the shield, for example, in the opening run of prayers. Sometimes it is a verbal echo, or an ancient heading which gives a clue. Such tradition must be taken seriously. I have before expressed my deep conviction that, in literary and historical criticism, a tradition has the first right to a hearing, and is to be expelled from the investigation only on proof of unreliability.

Psalm 3, for example was ascribed in very ancient times to a certain author on a certain historical occasion. The next three psalms follow because certain verbal echoes suggest a sequence. But that sequence is supported by the clear evidence of one developing theme. There is also a suggestion of a rhythm of morning and evening and again morning and evening, and a bonded sequence which envelops Psalms 2, 3, 4, 5, 6, and 23.

Hence the first small piece of writing which I found emerge from the weekly study of the Psalms. A career in free-lance journalism, as all who know me know, has been one of the real pleasures of my life, developed when doldrum years in the University were inadequate, for all the opportunity they supplied for enormously wide reading, to absorb all my energies. Few of my thoughts and activities do not ultimately emerge in the column I have written for the daily press under the name of Grammaticus. It has not missed a week for 42 years.

Hence the little book I produced in 1970, called *The Psalms of the Great Rebellion*. It was absorbed seven years later in the two volume commentary on the Psalms, which I produced for Scripture Union, but it gave me a little satisfaction to write it on the grounds I mentioned. I like to publish what interests and excites me, and have so far found publishers who have given me kindly aid and opening.

I added boldly the most famous psalm of all to the list because, if the earlier prayers marked the king's dogged retreat to Jordan and the rallying point at Mahanaim, surely only Barzillai's loyal reception to his king could account for the dual imagery of that small gem of poetry – the shepherd host. One stupid commentator actually finds fault with this, and divides the Shepherd Psalm into two basic documents. Talk of 'fern seed and elephants'!

I called the little book 'an imaginative exposition', possibly, I said, depriving a common class of reviewers of material for that third paragraph. In all my comments on the psalms of 1977, that same caveat applies. There is no harm in using a disciplined imagination, so long as one does not confuse speculation with assured conclusions, nor override the obvious in making a cherished theory sound more plausible.

In the smaller book I tried to locate biographically, and so illuminate a small tract of psalms, and I did so because I seemed, as I read the Psalter to be making the acquaintance of an anonymous scholar whom I have called 'the Anthologist', that rabbi of the Exile who, I think, played a vital part in the assembling of all the Psalms and also adding to the collection. I must speak more of him presently, because, if I am right in postulating his existence, he is one of the important figures in literary and religious history.

Those Psalms of David's second period of writing, when the deep shock of Absalom's rebellion shook him from his torpor of mind and soul, turned me to⸱ the quest for biography in all the Psalter, and this tuned well with the whole attitude to ancient literature which was my life's preoccupation. 'There is properly no history', wrote Emerson once, 'only biography'. He was repeated almost word for word, in similar contradiction of the monstrous historical theories of Karl Marx, by his two English contemporaries, Benjamin Disraeli and Thomas Carlyle. Hence my zeal to probe for the mind behind the Psalms. Hence, too, the admission that all those zealous for anything in learning must make, that final truth may have eluded their enthusiasm.

From my habitual biographical approach to literature and history, arose the awareness which I have just expressed of a personality behind the Psalms, 'the Anthologist' as I have just called him. It seems to me that the gigantic tragedy of the Exile, and the transportation of whole populations to Babylon, drove the survivors to the Book. The policy of the great imperialist and megalomaniac, Nebuchadrezzar, was neither genocide nor, as with the Romans, enslavement. His uprooting of the more useful members of subjected communities was to build a yet vaster metropolis – 'this great Babylon which I have builded'. Whole contingents were no doubt used and organised to extend the complex of irrigation works on which the administrative centre depended. Jonah described Nineveh, whose policies Babylon inherited, as 'three days' journey across', and the Chebar Canal, where Ezekiel visited a labour camp of deported Jews, was a scene of forced toil. But both the books of Esther and Daniel indicate that, compromising or fiercely retentive of their liberty, the Jews had a measure of freedom and no little opportunity before them. Ezra and Nehemiah suggest that a Remnant became an influential minority in the land of their captivity.

What held them together? Their geographical seat, their 'Holy Land', was gone. Their temple was destroyed. Their ritual of worship and the system of sacrifices was gone with the shrine. Their land was lamentably desolate as the records of the returning exiles show. They had only their book. Their early history stood recorded. They had the words of their great preexilic prophets, but it is a significant fact that when they came back to rebuild painfully their land, the Old Testament was largely written, a fact, to be sure, widely denied by the more determined of Old Testament liberals still, but on grounds as unsteady as most of their speculations.

Who organised this devotion to the Scriptures? Such zeal

led in the long course of time, to the extravagant bibliolatry of the scribes and the Pharisees, but let it not be forgotten that it was devoted men who jealously collected from a thousand memories the Psalms already written, who wrote, collected, stored the Scriptures, and so ensured the survival of their race.

They met and worshipped, and one cameo drama in the Psalms is a picture of them engaged in their perilous devotions. They were free, it seems, given the will, to organise their communal worship. Look at the strange and devastating Psalm 137. The little poem begins quietly with some exiled Jews meeting, as expatriates did (compare those of the town of Philippi five or six centuries later) by the river, here the willow-lined Euphrates. A sneering, alien crowd gathered round, saw their musical instruments hanging on the trees, and called for a song. The tiny synagogue was in no mood to make music for those who had caused their pain and trampled Jerusalem. They had one refuge, that of a 'commination' or a curse. There is actually a commination, set down for Ash Wednesday, in the Book of Common Prayer. It is seldom used, but helps to explain the background of the formal curse in an eastern context. A ritual commination thus appears in the little real-life drama of this psalm, the only hope a little band of worshippers had against brutal assault and perhaps drowning in the Euphrates.

Hence the sudden switch of the words, without intervening preamble, into fierce denunciation, as the Jews called down upon their Babylonian persecutors the horrors which the brutal city had inflicted on Jerusalem. When, a century ago, the distinguished Cambridge Arabic scholar, Professor G. H. Palmer, was murdered by Arab bandits in the Sinai desert, he is said to have invoked chilling horrors of retribution on his savage captors. It was his last effort to save his life. A curse, to an Oriental, is a most solemn and awful thing, loaded with foreboding, and full of a haunting power to pursue its victim to death. It is like 'pointing the bone' in Australian aboriginal lore. The one thus cursed dies. It lies on a guilty mind day and night, maddens and kills . . . But this digression is one of a hundred illuminating insights which came with a deep preoccupation with the Psalter, and is set out merely to demonstrate that the preoccupation I venture to postulate with the collection and preservation of the Scriptures, and the building of the Psalms into a coherent whole, was an organised project, and I like to imagine a skilled and sensitive rabbi in command.

I seemed to become peculiarly aware of him in the later parts of the collection, to see a mind at work, using, sorting and arranging as Moses did, already existing material. Our editor had some small collections at hand, the 'Egyptian Hallel', as Psalms 113 and 118 were called, and the 'Great Hallel', Psalms 120 and 136. Within these collections lay 'the Songs of Ascent', showing that the big task spilled over into the days of restoration. Book 5 of the Psalter became, more than the rest, the hymn-book of the new temple, which rose among Jerusalem's ruins with such pain and soul-searching.

The man who put the whole collection together, adding judiciously to the smaller assemblages some poems of David which had been omitted from the first four books, but which may have meant much to him personally, perhaps decided that he would divide Book 5 into two by a collection of his own. Hence Psalm 119, longest of all, reflecting what the word of God was coming to mean to him and his community in that time of national trauma. One can imagine his collecting from all quarters among the exiles, sayings and small poems, rhythmic in ideas as all Hebrew poetry was, varied tributes to the Law. Picture him writing some of those sayings himself, arranging them for memorising (that neglected and how salutary a practice!) in groups of eight under the 22 letters of the Hebrew alphabet, grouping them round some central thought or pursuing some process of thought. I found it, over many weeks I spent lecturing on that one psalm, a study of some delicacy to read until the patterns of its thinking and devotion became real and significant to me.

It is interesting to probe in the same context for the

personality and experience of the man. Run over some of its verses. He had known persecution, that most hideous of man's sins (22, 23); he had suffered under the heavy or the ruthless hand of authority, as Christians (and Jews) still do in the lands where the blanket of the dark has fallen (61,69). His faith had staggered under the load of it all (6, 22, 31). He had known pressure to give in and conform, as Daniel and his friends must have known. As alien Jew Mordecai and his loyally obedient niece demonstrated, there were prizes for Jews, always a clever and adaptable people, who chose to seek a place in the sun in an affluent society, and give up their long lamentation for a calcined ruin called Jerusalem. Our anthologist understood the temptation but was distressed that it should even brush his mind. The third section (gimel) seems particularly autobiographical. The writer had known deprivation and fear for his life (17), the dryness of soul of which Cowper wrote ('where is the blessedness I knew . . .') when the word itself seems to lose its savour (18) under the stress of life. He had known loneliness and rejection (19), the agony of seeming abandonment (20, 'my soul yearns all the time for thee to intervene', as Moffatt renders it). He sees hope glimmer in answer to his prayer (21), and claims reward for steadfastness. He had 'kept the faith' (22), even in the face of powerful contempt (23). He has already said that steadfastness is the key to happiness (4), and to remain steadfast a healthy fear of falling should be lodged in the mind (5, 6), for the peril is diminished only when the life's commitment and first vows are remembered (7, 8).

A man seemed to emerge through the mist of words as I peered into this long psalm, whose wealth is so often passed by, a man I seemed to know and understand. When I turned again to the earlier psalms as I undertook later the task of the commentary, I seemed, in the light of the acquaintance to understand more about them. I saw, for example, the reasoning for beginning with Psalm 2 on the turmoil of affairs, national and international, and proceeding with a sequence on David's second exile from Jerusalem. It was traumatic experience which an exile himself understood.

It also seemed clear to me that the first of all the psalms must have been written last by the Anthologist, as an introduction to the whole collection. Perhaps his description of blessedness and the 'happy' man (the adjective is too weak), indicates that the last touches were given to his immense task of collection, collation and arrangement, when the long banishment from the Land was over. And so he set to work and poured his best gifts into a final contribution. The whole psalm is a contrast of good and evil in the personality and experience of man, but in the first verse this master of formal Hebrew poetry develops a word pattern of three times three: walks, counsel, wicked; stands, way, sinners; sits, seats, scoffers. Not only is the ninefold word structure ornamental, but it is also true to psychological and spiritual experience, revealing the processes of backsliding in heart and mind. This he had fought in his own personal conflict.

Imagination, guesswork? Surely. But imagination, as I said, under some proper rigour of discipline, can be a pathway to fuller understanding. This was the lesson of the Psalms to me over a satisfying tract of life. I sought out every relevant historical fact available, related it all to life, avoided, I hope, all suggestion of dogmatism, and sought to share with others what the Psalms had to say preeminently to me. They can thus speak to all.

The Psalter, after all, is lyric poetry and such poetry is the language in which man expresses his wonder, love, passion, pain and praise. Lyric poetry in other literatures is preoccupied with more earthly emotions. The Hebrew Psalter is the lyric expression of man's wonder too, but also of his frustration, bewilderment, agony over sin, doubt and triumph over doubt, his desolation in the face of God's seeming inactivity and his triumph when God acts. The expression of it all is astoundingly frank. The Psalms bring to the feet of God our sorrow, sin and care. They give language to our prayers when our own tongue stumbles, coherence and point to our own unshaped aspirations.

They so often, I have found, provide a framework for our meditations, leaving us to fill in an absent phrase. Consider the subordinate clause at the end of Psalm 27. 'Unless I had believed to see the goodness of the Lord in the land of the living . . .' No more. The KJV translator's italicised 'I had fainted,' could hardly be more infelicitous. It is a most effective rhetorical aposiopesis, or sudden silencing, as effective as Moses' prayer under Sinai: 'Yet now, if thou wilt forgive their sin . . .' We are left in the prayer of David to fill in what our own desperate act, our own catastrophe of soul would be unless, not in some unimaginable paradise, but here, in the land of the living, we could see, in all circumstance, the outworking of a great, benevolent plan.

No less infelicitous, but grammatically more difficult to dispense with, is the italicised intrusion of 'it' in 37:5, ten psalms further on. There is a gap which we can fill in according to our own needs, with whatever is our 'daily bread' on the occasion.

Yes, I found the Psalms stimulate spiritual insight and crystallise experience. I am glad sometimes of a literal translation, like the expression in Psalm 4 with God as 'the lifter up of my head', or with the simplicity of 9:10 if one sifts the Hebrew metaphor: 'those who know what thou art can trust thee . . .'

But enough. I am not writing a mini-commentary on the Psalter. I simply tell what it meant over years of close familiarity, an experience many have shared. It is probably one of those far purposes destined to remain unfulfilled, like reading Gibbon right through, or filling in all the gaps in one's Shakespeare, but, if ever the day comes when I can read Hebrew more fluently, I shall go word by word through the Psalms as they were first written. I have discovered, in odd corners, enough to know that it would be a task infinitely rewarding.

8: The Bible as One Book

Prominent and immensely instructive among my experiences with the Bible must be listed the four occasions in which I have lived with the Book in its sequence and totality. I have been called upon in my career as a writer on such themes, to traverse the Bible carefully, and yet with varied purpose, four times.

Twice, over a period of five years, as a writer of the Daily Notes for Scripture Union, I went through the whole Bible, writing an average of 225 words daily, designed to instruct and to challenge, expository and devotional in their slant. The Scripture Union knew that I was not in agreement with their policy of covering the whole text of Scripture. Parts, though perhaps minor parts only, should have been reserved for what they called Study Notes. It was uncommonly difficult to extract a telling devotional comment, angled to haunt the thoughts throughout a busy day, from a passage, for example, of Levitical law, or from an obscure piece of apocalyptic poetry in Zechariah. Tradition prevailed, and I conformed.

The task had features not unlike those which attend the conscientious preparation of a sermon. The preacher who seeks to be something better than 'clanging cymbal or sounding brass', must move within the orbit of what he knows, and what he can from sincere experience say. But he must do more. As far as he can, he must envisage his audience, make some attempt to understand them, their needs, their capacities, and the truths for which they look. He must decide what he can best give, and what they should above all receive. I was aware that the Daily Notes in most cases were the material of morning devotion among thousands of busy people, caught in the rush of a great city's life, strap-hanging on the tube, packed in communter trains to Cannon Street or Charing Cross, shepherding in the Highlands, weaving the traffic on Sydney Harbour Bridge – a thousand situations before and during busy days. They even penetrated remote mission fields. I tried to share my own experience and knowledge relevantly and simply with them. But for over the five years of this unremitting activity, the writing of the notes directed much of my own day's thought and reading. They were written on planes and trains, in hospital beds, on holiday, and in the midst of crowded days, but mostly in bed before rising in the morning. One of the conveniences as 1963 ended the task, was the unimpeded access it gave to the vacuum cleaner underneath my bed. Usually a relevant commentary or two were stacked there, so that when the day dawned I could lean over, reach the books, read a little, and write the note for the day.

Those notes were thus my constant companion and led me into all manner of discovery. They were woven into the experience of life and have sometimes drawn meaning from trial and suffering. A rough path is sometimes worth the treading if, in so doing, we can tread down the brambles in the path of another. Hundreds of letters from all corners of the world spoke of this function, and gave me vast encouragement. They came in hundreds when I said good-bye, and touched the depths of my gratitude.

My second traverse of the whole range of Scripture was a decade later when I wrote, also for Scripture Union, the 740 studies on the characters of the Bible, personal and collective. Such a task involved me with great men, Abraham, Moses, David, Paul, Peter – Abraham daunting in his vision of the task which obsessed him, the gift, no less of a true God, a holy God to the world of man; Moses, heir of two cultures, nobly surrendering all to free a nation and give them, along with liberty, justice, a destiny and a vision; David, poetic, passionate, rising to sublime heights of insight and faith, tumbling to nether hells; Paul, one of all history's massive intellects, who knew how to weave the legacy of three dynamic peoples into a single culture, and a unique cementing faith; Peter, a fisherman, faulty, human, who led a band of simple men towards the conquest of the world . . .

And I met lesser men. Could less be said than in a sentence is said, of Enoch and Demas? A sentence, a mere noun and a verb is all most men need to tell all that need be told. Only the truly extraordinary need a paragraph. The whole task showed me the Bible, displaying two millennia of men and women, creatures like ourselves, the sorry raw material out of which God works his purposes. The very genealogies of Christ, standing awesomely, above, apart, and yet a part, of the whole marching throng, contain the persons of man's faultiest . . .

I observed the ruthless truth with which the Bible, from the patriarchs to the apostles, recorded them, making one and all recognisable in their flawed, as well as in the noble shapes and colours, of their humanity. It became as I read and wrote my 425 words on each, or on one facet of each man and woman, another demonstration of the Book's true humanity . . .

My fourth encounter with the Word as a whole, in its sweep, its complexity and its strange unity, came with the invitation to write first a one-volume commentary on the New Testament, and then an introduction (a 'handbook') to the Bible as a whole. Neither were to be too large for convenient handling, too academic for lay use, or too short for usefulness.

The task involved the reading of each book again, those familiar to me and ready to my hand, and those which were, or had been, more remote from my preoccupations. There were limits, as there are in such tasks, necessarily set down by the programmes of publishers, and the writer's circumstances. I have always written quickly once I have secured a clear conspectus of a task before me, and in this special context, having read the book, I looked at relevant commentaries and background literature. Exhaustive in such research or revision I could not be, but I did examine again all controversial matters, I tried to fill gaps in my own knowledge, I explored the more recent contributions to archaeological literature, and in this was a little surprised to find how the field had extended since I acted as an archaeological editor for Zondervan's five-volume *Encyclopedia of the Bible*. 'Let knowledge grow from more to more', prayed Tennyson when he wrote the Prologue to *In Memoriam*, and it has thus grown over all the landscape of man's learning. I wrote the books in any order, for I find it a path to freshness in writing, not to stay too long with one aspect of a subject, too long, for example, with the Pentateuch, the Gospels, the Pastorals. This in no way interfered with the great overriding impression of One Mind at work in a wide variety of humankind.

Here was a nation born to destiny, bound together and to history by a task, born in liberty, falling, rising, failing, triumphing, shaped by suffering as well as by success, beating out a view of life, divided yet one, scattered yet united, the mother of great men living in the native land of Christ, the producer of the interwoven Testaments. True, one can follow the Greeks from Homer to Hellenism, from Athens to Alexandria, one can see both Achilles and Xenophon influence Alexander; Rome can be viewed from the claustrophobic drive from a Tiber enclave to an Empire stretching from Hadrian's Well to the Persian Gulf . . . but nothing parallels Abraham to Christ and their binding story.

This was my theme when I undertook the task of the Olivier Beguin Memorial Lecture in 1975. This annual oration and publication is in honour of the General Secretary of the Bible Society from 1949 to 1972. At the time I was New Zealand President, and gave the lecture in Melbourne, Canberra, Brisbane, Auckland, Wellington and Nelson. Its theme is always the authority and relevance of the Bible in the modern world, and in my treatment I summed up the impressions of the first three of what I have described as the 'traverses' of the full field of Scripture. A task of writing or of speaking of such a comprehensive nature is a challenge, and I look back on the experience of that winter as personally illuminating.

I began where the Bible begins with Genesis and the Creation. What do the opening chapters of the Bible say? They are probably documents of immense antiquity, for literary culture, as all archaeology has shown goes back to remote ages in the river civilisation of the Euphrates Valley. Who first grasped the grand and fertile notion of the uniqueness and holiness of one Almighty God? Or should it rather be said, to whom was it first revealed? It is the same truth seen from opposite ends. Revelation comes by grace to seeking and outreaching faith.

Abraham, at any rate, was the first exporter of the truth which fill the opening chapters of the Bible, and became part of the venerable store which Moses wove into the early fabric of the Pentateuch. Read even in a remote translation, those pages of ancient literature are clothed with dignity and authority. If one sets the reserved Creation Story beside the grotesque myths of Sumer, Akkad and Babylon, the worth and uniqueness of the Hebrew record is evident. The words are austerely chosen, and framed to enlighten an unscientific past equally with a scientific present. No date is recorded, no special mode of creation set forth, save that a progressive sequence of life shows a majestic movement from primal chaos to conscious and responsible life. Man is set in a Paradise, in order, as the Hebrew says, 'to serve it', a plain phrase of which all the versions seem afraid, relevant though it is to our damaged planet. We have, then, the first creature to be called truly man, conscious of himself, his creator, of his freewill and his responsibility, living in a fruitful unpolluted world, tilling its rich soil, and serving it as it served him. Such a picture rings with truth.

To shift the focus to the world as man has made it, is to be faced with the simple conclusion that, at some point in his history, man of his free choice turned to disobedience and tore the delicate fabric of which he was a conscious and essential part. Canon Pearce of Norwich, who is an eminent anthropologist rightly maintains that the opening chapters of Genesis are an accurate account in the language of their antiquity, of what perceptive anthropology and archaeology may reasonably reconstruct of what is sometimes, a little awkwardly called 'prehistory' – the failure of emerging man to keep the peace, the collapse of collective politics, global catastrophe, they all crowd that distant record with sad familiarity. The style is clipped and crabbed, perhaps because of the recalcitrance of the writing material, the clay tablet. With the twelfth and subsequent chapters the story opens and flows, perhaps with the revolutionary emergence of the papyrus.

A sweep of history begins when a supremely great man invades the scene. Abraham sought God, and so was called by God to secede from a corrupt urban civilisation, the centre, in fact, of the world's trade and communications, Ur on the Persian Gulf, to found a nation which could carry, shape and deliver to a boundless posterity, the message of the One Holy God, to be set in opposition, contradiction and power against the foul cults which Abraham encountered in a world of which a great seaport was conscious, the animal obscenities and the priestly tyrannies which stretched as far east and west as the caravan trails and the long seaways ran. His vision was a people of God.

But visions do not always lie within reach of the first bold grasp. The great migrant became a shepherd-prince, and precariously, stumblingly, son and grandson sought to pursue the first sharp vision. It almost died in gloom and forgetfulness with the patriarchs, another generation on. Calmly, and with steady movement the story records their faulty humanity, their tragic errors, their sins and folly. Literary charm (witness Isaac's bride and Joseph's story), insight (Jacob's devious striving) and vivid characterisation, mark the story. Archaeology has strikingly illuminated the story. It is a true picture of life in Palestine, the petty kings, the clashing frontiers, the fight for water, the intruding Europeans from what we now call the Gaza Strip with Egypt ever perilously in the rear. The last chapters, perhaps recorded by Joseph's scribes, are redolent of the huge Nile empire, too obviously paralleled by Egyptian documents to be fiction. They shine with reality.

Exodus begins in tragedy. It is another world, another Egypt. The founding fathers are gone. The tribes, trapped in an alien land, serve the foreigner. Hope of Abraham's vision seems gone for ever. And then, as so often in history, some new force intrudes. Kipling put it well in the last stanza of *The Dawn Wind:*

'So when the world is asleep and there seems no hope of her waking
Out of some long, bad dream that makes her mutter and moan,
Suddenly, all men arise to the sound of fetters breaking,
And every man smiles at his neighbour and tells him his soul is his own'.

The 'new force' is likely to flow through the genius, the devotion, the dynamic personality of one man, an Abraham, an Alexander, an Augustus, unheralded, unexpected. Of such was Moses, a Hebrew, seemingly sequestered, educated, trained for leadership in the very precincts of Pharaoh's royal house. But how human the story of this giant among men, who wrenched a whole nation from their archipelago of labour camps, hammered them into unity, and gave them a symbolic ritual and a code of law. He failed at first, and in classic illustration of Toynbee's doctrine of Withdrawal and Return, a process which he reproduced in the very history of his people, he made an enormous stride towards the fulfilment of his spiritual legacy – Abraham's dream of a nation, with a message to carry.

To come thus, in one tract of reading, covering centuries of time, upon the books of the Law, is to see the strange unity in a handful of books so disparate. Consider Moses' monumental task. He proposed to settle in ancestral territory, now occupied by the related Canaanitish warlords, each in such bristling fortress sites as Hazor, Megiddo and Jerusalem, and considered an Egyptian buffer state, as Russian satellites might be viewed today, a people brutalised and cowed by the dominance of a great imperial power. He had to train them to believe in one God, and the ten plagues which lashed Egyptian pagan deities had helped in that;

but more, he had to wind that purifying faith into the fabric of their social and personal lives, to build again their sense of sin and conscience, and to realise that each held a responsibility to the power which had preserved them.

How far the tribes were from such a concept was demonstrated under erupting Sinai, when, with Moses' hand removed, the host lapsed into the unclean worship which was part of the way of life they had witnessed among their recent slave-masters. They built a representation of the Bull God, Apis, called it by another name, and staged a festival of ritual promiscuity. Hence, and this becomes clear on a continuous reading, the chapters which follow in this book and the rest of the Pentateuch with their code of Law. It was not the first human legal codes, but the first to be alive with a new conception of God. But along with the moral code went something more – a ritual of symbolic significance.

Under educative discipline, the tribes were taught to build, in minute detail, a lovely tent to speak of God's silent and unseen presence, One sitting on a 'mercy seat' over the tablets of the law, invisible but truly there, with divine beings gazing on the sprinkle of sacrifical blood and moral obligation. This is 'typology' sanctified by the New Testament, as are the services of the Tent, and does not sanction the imaginative extravagance of some who have spoiled the central solemnity and beauty of the whole by speculations on material, ropes, colours and minor architectural detail.

There came simultaneously the rules of sacrifice and offering, social, hygienic, didactic, theological, which taught that life was a network of choice between right and wrong, that sin and death were inseparably linked, that the clean and the unclean were a daily confrontation, under the scrutiny of a holy God. Daily obligation of such sort penetrates the soul, fashions the very vocabulary, and it provided a language of faith and religion which is still in use today.

Moses stands out as a giant of history and his dominating personality runs through four books. It forms a coherent theme amid their varied, historical, religious, moral and liturgical material. Winston Churchill, in a little known essay, recognised a kinship with him, Alfred de Vigny, my favourite nineteenth century French poet, wrote exquisitely of him with the theme of the desolation and loneliness of the great. It was an experience not to be forgotten to go with him, in my second 'traverse' of the Bible, and to see the majestic Pentateuch take coherent shape in his superbly educated mind and skilful hands.

But what of the painful reading for this violent war-ridden age in the books which follow? The stream of ben-eficient history, which began at Ur with Abraham, seems sunken to a mere rill, and yet nothing more important for the future of human history was happening in the world in those shocking centuries of the conquest of Canaan, and the agony of the era of the Judges, as the nation, so pre-cariously born in travail, struggled for coherence.

Looked at steadily, the people of Canaan, Sodom, Go-morrah and the rest could expect no more from the oper-ation of the moral law which runs through history, than the loathsome crops they had sown. The land had been overdue for sanitation for centuries. Societies so debased, sadistic, violent, sexually perverted, be they of the long distant past or of today, can hope for no more than they merit.

The crushed bones of infant offerings lie under the foun-dations of city gates. Great keeps speak of arrogant tyran-nies and bloody oppression. There are disgusting memorials everywhere of obscene cults. As one archaeologist has re-marked, the wonder is not that sentence fell on such a 'culture', but that its pollution was allowed to poison the land for so long.

The old vision was never lost. It emerges in the midst of stir and tumult, sometimes barely glimpsed, often in the strangest hands. There is always a remnant which remem-bers, a principle which was written, which perhaps still runs, through all history, always a Hand which seems to touch some willing man. History streams on to the century of unity under David, the poet-king, and the Golden Age of Solomon, if it may indeed be a time of golden years when wealth accumulates and men decay, moves on to what seemed final disaster with the land's division and the rise of the northern empires to match an imperial Egypt in the south. The land of Israel was pressed, as much of the world seems to be today, between mighty military powers, with whom all must take sides. The theme of prophet after prophet, for these godly men of insight and message arose in this period of unremitting fear and darkness to guide and encourage, was that God was still in control of history, and that catastrophe, if catastrophe should be permitted by him, was malleable and fruitful in his hands.

There came Assyria with its ruthless kings, Babylon the great aggressor, genocidal deportations, a trampled, ruined land, and out of such monumental disaster a reborn people, welded, as the first captivity had welded them, into one, a people that had discovered its Book and still clung to its destiny. Behind the frontiers of fear, as Israel still knows them, like the cohort camps round Masada, the prophets taught and preached. There is nothing in literature quite like those great interpreters. They came from all ranks of life, Amos the peasant breaking into the corrupt court like Elijah before him, to cry for justice and denounce corruption, Isaiah the aristocrat, holding a people firm by the magnificence of his oratory and the power of his faith, as the armoured host of Sennacherib, with the black smoke of burning crops and villages behind them, rolled down on Jerusalem, Isaiah, whose deep pondering on God's ways, broke through the gossamer web of time, and saw the Coming One, the Suffering Servant, 'scorned and rejected of men', and yet the final giver of the peace for which a harassed world still yearns. There was Jeremiah, the son of the priest of Anathoth, from the little village where the forbidding hills of Judaea shelve down towards the Jordan, Jeremiah called to supervise surrender, so bitterly remote from Isaiah's task to stand firm and resist, but whose pain foreshadowed the very sufferings of Christ. So with the rest. It was a fascinating task, when I was analysing the characters and personalities of the Bible, to place the prophets in the historical setting of the historical books, to note their rôle with the anonymous historians, and see them as the remote interpreters of history, the ancestors of Herodotus, Spengler, Toynbee.

I found the same understanding, the same anguish, and insight into the ways of man in the terse wisdom of Proverbs, the poignant questioning of Job into what seemed meaningless disaster . . . The Psalms as a personal experience I have already spoken about . . .

And the Old Testament cannot be divided from the New. Extract the Old Testament from the century long documents of the book which was its consummation, and the sorriest tatters will be left. It is almost a century from the birth of Christ to the death, in extreme old age, of John, the last of the apostles. Its theme is God's intrusion into history, of God's Person, his 'only begotten son', the narratives of his followers, the Passion story – but this needs no repetition. In all three or four readings of the whole Bible my task here merged, and I was also on my common ground with ancient Greek and Roman history, for I have explained how I had learned to approach the New Testament as a unique collection of first century documents – and on that century I have read and written much. It is good to discover unity in the mind.

The Bible and I – full length on four different paths. I saw in those encounters, a sort of Emmaus walk, some deep truths, how inspiration, for example works – a divine encounter between the communicating Spirit of God, and the utterly surrendered mind and heart of a human being willing to be used. God, in fact, only uses that which is surrendered to him, some loaves and fishes equally with a brilliant mind, an experience of agony as in Psalm 22, or an anguished repentance as in Psalm 51. John Ruskin once contemplated a mess of mud behind one of the hideous factories against which his artist's nature raged. He pictured the elements gathered there recast into nobler forms, not added to, not diminished, simply changed.

The clay, ridding itself of all foreign substance becomes a white earth, and aided by a congealing fire, emerges as the finest procelain. But leave it again to follow its own course, and it can become, as its atoms reassemble and align, clear and hard, and able to deal with light in a special way, gathering, such is its structure, the blue rays only. It is called sapphire.

The sand can follow a similar course. Its silica can outdo the achievement of the clay, and set themselves in such parallel lines that they can reflect not only blue, but green, purple and red, or, denying all access to its structure, become pure black. It is then called opal, of one hue or another.

And the soot there commingled. Under enormous pressure its plain carbon can be so metamorphosed that, in Ruskin's words, 'it wins the power of reflecting all the rays of the sun at once in the vividest blaze that any solid thing can shoot. We call it then a diamond.'

That was the lesson the Bible seemed to teach me. Man's experience can be so transformed. How human a book, yet how divine, showing man what God can make of man and in the act producing a book which speaks to man. There is no other way of reading it. The Bible is not a collection of obscure oracles, but a living entity, as Christ, its final theme and substance, was a living being, in which we discover our own selves. It is true that there is no substitue in the world of learning for staying with a small area of study until we have come as near to mastering it as the human mind, in any sphere, can come. But in the laudable pursuit of that process it must not be forgotten that the synoptic view is important too. We must see the theme in its wholeness.

Is not much of what I have said been a clear illustration of that fact? I have spoken of areas of intensive preoccupation and attention, John's writings, Luke's two books. I could add Peter, and just possibly the Psalms and Revelation, though some parts of that strange book still elude me. But I am also profoundly thankful for the obligation which fell on me to see it whole, in its sweep, its majesty and unity.

They miss much who seek only magic oracular tags in the Bible's pages. I heard of a man once who moved house every seven years because 'here we have no continuing city', and of another who was deeply disturbed at being in the police force because Paul, urging care in thrusting new converts into prominence, adjured Timothy, as the KJV puts it, to 'lay hands suddenly on no man.' There are, in fact, such persons whom the foes of conservatism call 'obscurantists', those who seek to obscure or darken. 'Informed conservatism', was the phrase I recommended, and it applies to the whole, as well as to the parts, of that wondrous collection of 775,693 words which we call the Bible. 'Pick it up and read it', was the cry which came across the hedge in the story of Augustine's conversion. It comes to everyone who seeks and honours truth.

9: The Bible and its landscape

In my introduction to Zondervan's Bible Atlas which I edited a decade ago, I quoted a quaint word from John Smith's *Generale Historie of Virginia:* '. . . as Geography without History seemeth a carkesse without motion, so History without Geography wandereth as a Vagrant without a certain habitation.' It is a true word, and a fact I was always careful to point out in lecturing on ancient history. Geography and history can scarcely be studied apart, take any land at any time.

So it is that the Bible cannot be dissociated from the land in which its story took shape and form. In teaching the history of Greece I always showed how the configuration of the land, the fertile valleys and plains cut up by dividing hills, the intruding sea, the islands and the proximity of the great blunt peninsula which Asia thrusts towards Europe, moulded the structure of Hellenic history, played a part in Greek thought, spawned statehood and forms of government . . .

Roman history was fashioned by Rome's search, and her ultimate failure to find a stable frontier, within the physical limits of her reach, from the group of hill-forts at the Tiber ford to an empire, which formed, even at its greatest, no more than a rim of lands precariously held by the legions and their military roads. It ran only from northern Britain, along the Rhine and Danube, Europe's longest river-line, to the Euphrates where the gap was never closed, and then south, perilously ill-defined, round the inner rim of the 'Fertile Crescent', to the valley of the Nile.

It was in the middle thirties that I discovered among the

books I acquired from J. W. Kemp's library, George Adam Smith's *Historical Geography of the Holy Land*. When Allenby was boarding the train at Victoria to begin the liberation of Palestine from the Turk, in 1917, Lloyd George hurried down the platform with that fine volume in his hands. The bulk of the work is still valid, though the Middle East, especially Israel, has changed beyond recognition in 80 years. The deserts blossom, as the prophets once promised. The Jordan river plain, if only peace could come with the sharing of water and the obliteration of frontiers of strife, could alone supply all Europe with winter vegetables.

But it is the more profound insights of the great geographer which so impressed me. There is a passage which points out how the Holy Land, of all places on earth, was the one spot where a nation could grow and cohere, and experience history in the way that Israel did, beating out in the process the Old Testament. The land is a confluence of nations, a meeting ground of empires, lying in the crossroads of three continents, at once a sanctuary and an observatory, solving the problems of suffering and strife, gathering force and deepening understanding of the ways of men, until, in the fulness of times, it gave Christ to the world.

It was delightful to meet such understanding of the ideas I was myself forming as a teacher of classics, and I looked forward to the time when I should myself see the contours of the lands of the Bible. The deepening darkness of the times, the looming war, and the years of war's horror postponed that day. It came, and for 10 whole years of my retirement, travel has been a flood of meaningful experience, as I have annually led tours to the Mediterranean and the Middle East. There were days of easier access. Lebanon was a place of tranquillity and peace. The West Bank was once less full of fury, and one could drink the clean cold water of Jacob's well with no fear of gunblasts in Nablus up the road. One decade of visits saw immeasurable change, but there are places, which cannot change, from the waters of Galilee and the hot sun springing up from the Golan

Heights, to the grim and bloodied keep of Masada above the cruel hard sea. We drank to the full the land's romance, reality and meaning.

Let me lift that one word 'reality'. One understands better on the spot. It was strange to speak to a convention of Christian Arabs and Israelis at a meeting place on Carmel at Easter time almost 20 years ago, to hear Isaiah 53 read in Hebrew, and to read aloud from Mark's Greek the story of Calvary, and then to clamber through the scrub below the Carmelite monastery and see the theatre in the hillside where Elijah confronted the Baal priests.

The chanted invocation seemed to quiver in the air. It was and is a magnificent view past the willow-lined Kishon at our feet across the tesselated Esdraelon Plain to the hills of Galilee, and see the edge of the steep where Nazareth stands 20 miles away. It was thence, perhaps that Christ stood looking southwest towards us when, 'from a high mountain', he saw 'the kingdoms of the world'. For, in truth, one can. Thothmes the Third marched north that way to fight the Hittites on the Orontes in the campaign which stands depicted on his walls. Allenby took the pass of Megiddo, still guarded by its ruined Canaanite keep below us, and with its capture deemed his campaign ended. He named his earldom from the pass. Alexander, Antony, Napoleon, all passed that way. 'The kingdoms of this world', indeed.

But the strangest sight of all was when we climbed the hill behind, and saw the west wind driving cumulo-nimbus cloud in on the land. It was a cloud mass like an enormous hand, with five coiled thunderheads standing out of it like fingers. The Hebrew in that story simply says 'like a man's hand.' We were seeing what Elijah's boy saw, and it was a little uncanny, a giant's hand grasping.

It is always moving to look on Jerusalem from the Mount of Olives over whose shoulder the road, which descends 4000 feet to Jericho and the Dead Sea, passed. It is the long climb by which Christ came to the City to face the end, with his insensitive disciples quarrelling over precedence, and lagging behind him. It is a different view indeed from that on which Titus looked from his headquarters on Mount Scopus, where the great University stands and where New Zealanders lie in war graves today. Then as now the Old City lay across the dry Kidron Valley, tilted towards the olive-covered mountain, but, where the sun and the moonlight glitter today on the golden dome of Omar, and the silver dome of El Aksar, stood then the beauty of the Temple, white still from the chisels of Herod's masons, on the enormous platform which that scoundrel had sheathed in mighty stone to hold it. The gigantic blocks of the Wailing Wall are part of it still surviving, and form the scene of the continual prayers of the black-clothed Orthodox Jews, still unaware that their Messiah came – and went.

Layer on layer, filling onetime valleys and levelling hills, like modern Rome covering the hillforts of prehistory, Jerusalem is the piled mass of human toil, joy and sorrow going back to the mysterious monarch of Salem whose sanctity Abraham honoured with gifts and obeisance. To the right from the vantage point on the Mount of Olives lies the crag of Zion, city of David, captured dramatically from the Jebusites 3000 years ago. David's commandoes entered by such water tunnels as one can see on much larger scale in the forbidding strongholds of the Canaanites at Megiddo and Hazor. On the stony slope opposite, under the medieval walls, the archaeologists have identified fragments of Hezekiah's and Nehemiah's building. Almost undoubtedly, the name means 'City of Peace', but no comparable area is so soaked with the blood, sweat and tears of men. There is much in Jerusalem which most deeply stirs me, much which revolts. I shrink from the Church of the Holy Sepulchre with its five competing sects. I am moved to the heart to stand on the stones of the Pavement where Christ stood in his own blood, the butt of the legionaries' brutal play. The Stations of the Cross do not lift my soul, save that, whichever Via Dolorosa you choose, you may fairly guess that the path which the Lord trod is some 20 feet below. Old roads survive. I reserve my own reverence for the way through the Damascus Gate, and along the Nablus Road where the Garden Tomb in the venerable old close is cut into the ridge, which ends in the grim skull of Gordon's Calvary. Jerusalem seems so often sinister, but it is an experience which is woven with my understanding, a symbol in the mind as some historic places become from Troy to Gallipoli.

So it is with the gaunt fortress rock of Masada by the Dead Sea, where less than a thousand Jews beat off the Tenth Legion for three hopeless years after the fall of Jerusalem. This monument to desperate courage is not in the New Testament, but it does fulfil a dire warning of Christ about the violence which the men of blood were bringing on the land. It does stand for the mob's wild screaming for the resistance leader to be released to them, and the gentle Christ sent to his awful death. Unlike Jerusalem it may be seen naked to its hot rock foundations, its huge storage barns in black desolation, and its fortifications in battered ruin. One can walk up the ramp the Romans built, at the cost of a multitude of Jewish lives, and the sweat and blood of soldiers and slaves alike, when July and August brought the blazing sun to the superheated valley and the scorching khamsin blew. It stands a symbol which the Jews still recognise. Sharon's tank brigades swore their oath there: 'shenith Masada lô tipol' – Masada shall not fall again. It looks still, as it looked from the bend of the road west to Arad, when the general, Silva, turned in his saddle to look back at the mighty rock which had cost him so much to take, just to prove that Rome was lord of all, and which he took at last in eerie silence for all inside were dead, each destroying themselves and their own rather than fall alive into the hands of the invading conqueror. I am glad with a sombre satisfaction that I have clambered in the heat over that bloodstained outcrop and heard the still vibrating words of Eleazar ben-Yair: 'Now the time has come to do that which we have always determined we shall in such case do.' They did. Can one blame the Israeli, who looks down today on the circle of the ruined cohort camps, and through clenched teeth breathes: 'Masada shall not fall again'?

It is in the New Testament, a theme I have anticipated, that I find the Bible most fascinatingly welded to its landscape. I have already quoted Ernest Renan, the French Semitist and scholar of 120 years ago, who so fascinated me when I read French in the University as a boy. His scepticism did not shake me, in spite of my admiration for his lucid French, for I grasped promptly the ruinous prejudice which inhibited his processes of research. If one begins with a firm determination not to consider any statement of 'the miraculous', it is impossible to pursue some vital avenues of research. An arrogant assumption that what is 'miraculous' is capable of final definition, and rules out both presuppositions and conclusions which might be vital to an argument, can block paths to reason as well as to faith.

This was a pity with a mind like Renan's, but allow him to speak again of his visit in 1860 to Palestine: 'All this history which seemed to float in the clouds of an unreal world, took thus a form, a solidity which astonished me. The striking agreement of the texts and the places, the marvellous harmony of the evangelical idea and of the country which served it as a framework, were to me a revelation. Before my eyes I had a fifth Gospel, disfigured though still legible.' It is a pity a scholar so notable did not pursue his 'revelation', and reach the saving conclusion. One cannot surely follow truth hobbled by a prejudice which forbids following the way which the path leads. But with the tenor of the great writer's words, and the nature of his experience, I could not feel myself more in tune.

I treasure the quietness of Galilee. To be sure if one can visit the tiny corner of Gethsemane where the three large basilicas of the competing churches have permitted themselves to leave a few gnarled olive trunks, whose roots may have survived for 2000 years, one can shut the eyes, hear the song of a bird and the rustle of a leaf, and think that Christ heard those sounds. But in Galilee his sights and sounds are everywhere – in the lapping of the lakewater when one is far enough from shore to dim the noises of the land, the brushing of the wind down the westward funnel of the Tabgka vale, fanning the faces of those who once sat on the Mount of the Beatitudes, the silent curve of the bay in which, in more crowded days, he sat and spoke from a boat, surely the only possible place, for the voice is caught in a curve of shore and carried, as it is carried high in a Greek theatre, its ultimate whisper lifted to the very hilltop. Or stand in front of the synagogue, at Capernaum, where the floor would remain under its toppled stone when Hadrian destroyed it, and think that, on those flagstones, till the Vandal excavators broke them out for amulets and souvenirs, you were standing on the very stones where Christ stood, with the silver of the lake glittering through the leaves which screen the shore. Yes, Galilee is real and comes to life.

This is a theme which could long continue. Scene after scene tangles and blends in the memory with Scripture and Bible history, immortal saying and decisive event. 'On this rock . . .' said the Lord at Banyas in that dell of green where the major spring of the Jordan leaps from a cave in a crag. It is a formation which lucky travellers have seen far to the north behind Byblos, where the mightier Afqaa spring roars out in one leap amid the wheeling swallows just under the Lebanon snow. Banyas (or Caesarea Philippi) is a gentler spot, and the Israelis have done well not to destroy green trees just to see the mosaic floors of Philip's palace there. But to return: 'on this rock' – and there embedded in the golden-red rock is the back of an ancient temple of Pan. Banyas, of course, was where the goat-footed god was worshipped, and it gave Christ the illustration he was ever ready to pluck from what was around him. And can one who has seen it ever forget the scene when he reads? Or that of the well in Nazareth, if one was fortunate to see it, before someone had the insensitive notion to smother it with a church?

Or the Vale of Elah, where the stream through the narrow little beqaa, or valley plain, is full of stones, and where two battle-weary armies lined the ridge, and the huge swaggering hoplite, Goliath, came out to shout and to challenge? If only a week can be spared for Israel (no bigger than Vermont or Wales, if Sinai is left out) it is worth it. Of course, it is better if longer contact can be made with the land on foot, by a stay in a kibbutz, by more time simply to sit and stare, but as I have tried to show in a book (*Eight Days in Israel*), even a hurried and hustled visitor can bring away impressions which will not cease to sing in the memory. My own many visits of this sort, when time perhaps has been found to walk west down the Roman road through Emmaus, with a blazing, falling sun dazzling the eyes, right down to the low ruins of little houses, to pluck a fragment of pottery from a bank above the surf at Ashkelon, or eat in celebration with others from five small loaves and a couple of Galilee mullet on the grass behind En Gev under the Golan hills, these and a hundred other tiny cameos, remain a transforming memory. To read the Bible in its landscape, to translate aloud the story of the Samaritan woman at Sychar, the Beatitudes above the silver lake, Luke's story of Zacchaeus under the oranges and sycomores of Jericho, with the Mount of the Temptation stark across the river plain, has been to share such an experience which some have told me stays alive in the memory for the rest of life. To me it has been delight which has been like a late lark singing.

It must not be forgotten that the landscape of the Bible extends far beyond Israel. The Lord once went to Tyre, the patriarchs went to Egypt. The Church was planted in New Testament times from Antioch to Rome, and all have landscapes where word and event are mingled with its story. I have found enlightenment under the stimulus of a scene alive with reality in more than one place. Clambering with a grandaughter down the rough slopes of Patmos I remember once becoming suddenly aware that John was, as the Romans called it, 'relegated' to the island; he was not a convict in a labour camp. As we paused among the thorn bushes in that scrambling descent, we could hear the faint sighing of the surf round the island ('his voice was as the sound of many waters'); we could see the sloping sun to the west turning the whole Aegean into molten gold, like fire commingled with the sea, another image from the Apocalypse. A tall mountain of cumulo-nimbus intershot with lightning and quivers of green, red and steely-blue, stood high to the east, reverberated with thunder, and filled the still air with murmurs of menace. It sent splats and splots on the path at our feet. It was exactly the throne of God in Revelation. Indeed the whole place seemed full of the imagery of John's book.

It suddenly struck me with force, seeing thus the Apocalypse 'in its landscape', that John had the run of the island. Any senatorial governor of Asia had no reason to love 'the bald Nero', Domitian, who was equally raging in fear against the senators and the Christians. A hint in Peter's letter, indeed, might suggest that Christians, who had infiltrated the imperial family, were not without implication in the plots against the sadistic emperor. Christians were involved against Hitler, after all.

Since, long before, the custodians of the imperial cult, 'the Asiarchs' or 'rulers of Asia', had skilfully covered the withdrawal of Paul from Ephesus, is it not as likely that a governor of Asia might scatter the Christians, up the radiating river valleys, to the islands, before he made a show of obeying an imperial order to persecute? The river plains were full of churches, even in Paul's day. You can sit on the white silica-coated cliff where the sickly warm water runs down from basin to gleaming basin, giving point to John's letter to the congregation at Laodicea, and can see within the sweep of the eye the site of Hierapolis, the site of Colossae, the site of Laodicea, as close as any three modern suburban churches. Almost in view is the recently excavated Aphrodisias, soon to be the see of a bishop. We seldom realise how thick the Christians were upon the ground until we visit the old province of Asia at the south-western end of the peninsula.

It was William Ramsay, whose *Letters to the Seven Churches,* was an acquisition from Kemp's rich library, which first made me aware how open and plain those apocalyptic epistles were, when subjected to the scrutiny and the enlightenment of their own geography, tradition, history, coinage and the epigraphy so widely restored by archaeological investigation. I have been round them three times, and especially at Pergamum and Ephesus, widely deepened my understanding by walking over their sites and pondering their landscape.

Ephesus is by way of being the largest archaeological remain to be found in New Testament contexts. Acts 19 comes vividly alive there, and I have more than once amused myself and, I hope, made the famous story of the riot more clear, by dramatising Luke's brilliantly told story. It is easy to persuade a crowd to enter into the spirit of the rhythmic chant: 'megalê hê Artemis tôn Ephesiôn' with hand-clapping and din, and then assume the role of the city official, anxious for Ephesus' status as a 'free city' under the jealous eye of the Roman authorities, subtly quieting the enflamed mob. People are not interested in statistics, nor in too many dates, when, for example, Wood found the theatre over a century ago, nor when Domitian built it. They are fascinated by the human story. All the parties stringing round the tourist walk once joined me, without any opposition from the bored Turkish guides.

One sees, too, what seems, so unaccountably at times, to escape the interest of those who write about and photograph the scene. On a high relief by the theatre gate is a carving of a Roman legionary in battle gear and in a fighting stance. Paul must have seen the sculpture every day, and have drawn from the sharp recollection the sustained metaphor of the sixth chapter of his Ephesian letter, the warrior of Christ in his spiritual battlefield, arrayed in the whole panoply of God.

Corinth offers a stage as dramatic. Gallio, gentlemanly brother of Seneca, had his Achaean headquarters in the city of the Isthmus, when he was governor of the province. It is interesting to mount the judge's 'bêma', at the end of the forum, to read Gallio's stern words in their ancient language, to translate them, and then to tell those standing below to do what Paul, unaccustomedly silenced, was surely thankful and prompt to do – turn quickly away and go. What did he immediately see? He saw eight remaining columns of a Doric temple to Apollo, surviving from the port which the Romans so brutally destroyed in 146 B.C. And, of course, you have forthwith the answer why, in his letters to Corinth Paul uses the imagery of the temple three times. There are swift scenes, caught by the eye in a moment of high intensity or crisis, which imprint themselves upon the brain for ever. Paul had such a moment before Gallio's judgment seat, when the officials of the synagogue, insensitively not seeing the need, after so recent an expulsion from Rome by Claudius, to keep 'a low profile', crowded clamouring round the bench of a Roman magistrate who had a high and proper appreciation of his functions in the place of justice.

We might first have stayed with Paul in Athens, where the New Testament gives a priceless picture of the wondrous city 500 years after the days of its glory, living on its academic reputation, on its tourist trade, and forming the haunt of fortune-hunters from cult to commerce. Paul's remarkable speech in which a perceptive student of Greek literature can pick up five literary allusions, comes to life in the topographical context of its utterance. The ancient court of the Areopagus (the knoll of Ares or Mars) had, it seems, in some form, jurisdiction over those who sought to lecture in Athens, and that jurisdiction was divided between the two philosophic schools which divided the academic world of the day. With Athenian polish and courtesy, the court invited the Jewish visitor to address them. He did so, of course, at much greater length than Luke's brilliant summary might suggest. His hearers responded variously, only one member of the august body before him with conviction, but they all evidently judged his approach sufficiently philosophical to merit their licence to preach.

I have stood on the flat-topped rocky outcrop and recited what he said. Indeed, in neat Greek lettering, a bronze plaque on the side of the hill displays it in Luke's Greek. But behind where the court sat, towers the greater outcrop, the Acropolis, still a wonder in its sad ruin. Imagine what it was like when Paul waved his hand towards its undamaged glory, the beautiful Parthenon, the delicate temple of the Wingless Victory, the two astonishing statues of Athena, and said to that tolerant audience: '. . . we ought not to think that God is like gold, silver or stone shaped by the clever art of man . . . being lord of heaven and earth, he does not live in temples made with hands . . .' The speech, in its landscape, sounds different. I have preached on the theme in the little Greek Evangelical Church opposite Hadrian's Arch, and found the congregation delighted to hear their language read in its ancient form from my Greek Testament.

But illustrations on the subject could clog the chapter. Just as Joseph's story, they tell me, comes to life in Egypt, so the early Church assumes sombre reality in Rome's Catacombs, which were first being cut in the papa rock under the Eternal City before the last apostle was dead, and in the scene of the little 'house meeting' with the cross on the wall in the ruins of Herculaneum, where Paul may have met the Christians on his way through Puteoli, 17 years before that day at the end of August, six weeks after Titus succeeded Vespasian, when the explosion of Vesuvius blotted out the towns along the Bay of Naples.

All writers, as Gilbert Highet, the classicist, showed in a charming book on the Augustan poets, can draw significance and illumination from the landscape which was their background, and so, preeminently, can the Bible, and my adventures with both Testaments would have lacked a whole dimension had I lacked opportunity to see and place them in the contexts, not only of their time, but that of their place.

The world closes in. I cannot now go to places where I have so freely been. I cannot explore Lebanon, where I once found such tranquillity from Tyre and Sidon to the Beqaa, and to Baalbek. I should hesitate to visit Belfast, much less Iran. I find myself uneasy in Rome and Naples, and especially Jordan, where Jerash, the 'far country' of the Prodigal Son, is more than worth a visit. I walk alone and leisurely no longer in many parts of the deteriorating world, in far too many places. Shall we instance the Delphi Museum, the very paths on Masada on a Jewish Sabbath, or Yad Vashem, where the tourist horde makes looking and strolling a weariness – or worse. Central Park is as unpleasant, it must be admitted, as an Arab suq in Nazareth, or a back-street in Old Jerusalem, all irksome or unhealthy places now.

For those who wish to see and to travel in historic lands, the area of comfort does not widen. I am glad I saw so much in quieter days. It has enriched my mind, and sharpened my understanding in all ancient literature, the sphere of a life-time's teaching, as well as the Bible. We still owe much to Sir George Adam Smith and his fellow knight, Sir William Ramsay. And not the least of the pleasure of it all was the duty I have so often assumed of imparting my accumulated information to intelligent groups of fellow-travellers.

10: The Book which understands

The final chapter of any book can be the most important as well as the latest to be written. That, I hope, could be as true of life itself. I have pondered long on what remains for me here to say. I have tried to show the unusual nature of my Biblical education, and how it has been a Christian byproduct of a rigorous training as a student and as a teacher of the two great classical literatures and two full millennia of ancient history, along with all which illuminates both.

But now, when I proceed to write with deeper personal intimacy of the Bible in the closer and more heartfelt experiences of life, I tread much more common ground with my fellows, for the Bible is itself much more than a book of scholarly preoccupation. It is part of God's self-revealing to man. The Son, as the last verse of John's immensely significant Prologue puts it, 'has explained' God. And more: it is the book which diagnoses the human condition, and which, quite beyond any other writing of man, tells us all of ourselves.

It was as I considered this thought that I remembered Emile Caillet's *Journey into Light*, lent to me by a good friend a decade ago, and fortunately still in his son's possession. It is a curious fact how a book, perhaps read casually at first, can at some proper time, assume significance. The great French scholar, who ended his academic career as Professor of Christian Philosophy at Princeton, provided me thus with the sentence for which my mind was groping.

Here is the story. Scarred and hurt by the horrors of the First War, where he was wounded almost to death in the trenches before Verdun, Caillet could find no place in his life for a faith, any spiritual dimension or practice of religion. He married a Christian woman, who, for all her Scottish and Irish ancestry, played the part of a good French wife, and passively accepted her husband's ban upon religion in their home.

Meanwhile he was not at peace, busy though his fine mind was in seeking for a meaning in that which we call life. He was unsatisfied and unfulfilled, a prime illustration of what Augustine said at the beginning of his *Confessions:* 'You have made us for yourself and our hearts find no rest until they find their rest in you'. Caillet read avidly in ancient and modern literature and philosophy, those wide tracts of human wisdom and experience in which my own youth and early manhood were involved – though I had faith not faithlessness. I knew the Bible. Caillet was blind to it.

By some strange blockage of the mind, he never looked at the Word of God, but felt that somewhere, there must have been put into compelling speech, wisdom which would bring peace out of his tumult of soul, purpose to answer his aimless confusion.

Caillet did what, with quite a different object, I have done. I have a small leather-bound pocket-book in which I write poetry in several languages which has moved me. He had such a book into which he transcribed passages which probed the mysteries of the spirit. He hoped that, when he had collected enough of the wise and penetrating utterances of men, he would have 'a book which would understand him', and lead finally from fear and anguish to release and tranquillity.

He remembers, he tells us, a hot summer day when, alone in his house, he sat in the garden with his book to read and to absorb. Instead of speaking to his condition, his extracts left him where he was, remembering only where he had discovered them, and why he had chosen them. The words carried no persuasion. They were simply the words of others like himself.

At the same hour, his wife was pushing a baby carriage around the streets of the little town. The cobbles were rough under wheels and feet. A tiny green garden-close glimpsed through an archway attracted her. On impulse she went in. Up a stone stairway she found a long room, and an old white-haired man sitting. She had stumbled on a Huguenot chapel, hidden thus since the days of persecution. She asked, and it felt as if she heard herself asking, for a Bible in French. She was given one and took it home.

For all his wide scholarship, her husband had never had a Bible in his hands. He took it to his room and opened it at random – at the Beatitudes. He read and read, and found satisfaction surge into his soul. He had found it – the book which understood him. And in the book he found the Christ who made it live.

The living Word is made alive by the Living Christ, and that is why the strange story of Emile Caillet's conversion speaks so loudly to my own spirit. In the Old Testament God announced himself to Moses as 'He who is'. In one of the Ras Shamra tablets he calls himself, as he might also have called himself in the Hebrew Scriptures, 'He who speaks'. Such a Bible our faith must have, or faith crumbles at its foundations. Such a Christ the Bible must have, or it withers into a collection of tragic documents. I have tried to say clearly in this book that I have been sure, since I became a Christian, that all faith must be based on a Word of Truth, a Word of Authority, and that, if Christ be not risen, we are indeed 'of all men most miserable' who have trusted him.

Just like John Bunyan in his *Grace Abounding*, we long for 'a word to lean on'. That is what stayed with me when I read that most moving of all Plato's dialogues, the *Phaedo*, which records the last conversation of Socrates with his friends. At sundown he was, by the mad court's decree, to drink the hemlock, and he spent his last hours piling reason on reasons to justify his belief in survival after death. He makes Simmias, one of the company sum up. 'A man must do one of two things; either he must learn or discover the truth about these matters, or, if that is impossible, he must take whatever human doctrine is best or hardest to disprove, and, embarking upon it as upon a raft sail upon it through life – unless he can sail upon some stronger vessel, some word of God and make his journey more safely and securely.'

Exactly Caillet's story. Exactly mine, and that is why I have, all my life, held fast to the Bible and its living Christ. I have done so, I claim, with the integrity proper to scholarship. I could not live easily with a divided mind. Indeed Scripture forbids precisely that. And I record my assurance again that the Bible is an act of God. God spoke in it, as the learned writer to the Hebrews said, 'in sundry times and divers manners' – over 2000 years, I believe, and through men as diverse as Amos the farm-labourer and the supremely learned Paul, the courtly Isaiah and fisherman John.

And let it be said here that stories like that of Caillet are not the norm. Enlightenment comes to all in different ways. Paul himself did not really come to Christ in a blaze of light near the place, perhaps, where Kuneitra stands today on the Golan road to Damascus. That was where he ceased to struggle against the memory of the stones dashing into Stephen's face outside the Jerusalem gate. Like C. S. Lewis he was dragged into the kingdom, though not, I think, as Lewis adds, the most unwilling convert in the land. To quote Caillet verbally: 'A pilgrim of goodwill is headed for a spiritual breakthrough. Not that the same be necessarily dramatic. The day it comes may be just another day. Even so it will in the long run be remembered as having made a fresh departure, as having imparted a new colour and warmth to the life of the wayfarer.' There is what the Fabians of the last century called the 'inevitability of gradualness'. So it was with Wesley who went to the Aldersgate prayer meeting 'very unwillingly', but found his heart 'strangely warmed'. So it has been with me.

'Jesus is Lord' may have been the earliest confession of faith of the Church. It is the beginning of all faith. The children in the first of Lewis' Narnia books, when they met again the great golden lion, Aslan, thought he had grown bigger. So does Christ to every dedicated Christian. There is no one else to preach, and it is the mark of every deviant liberal theology to make him ever smaller, and to reduce him to less daunting size. That is why it causes me sometimes to wonder how, with a Christ so immense, so many can say so much in the pulpit about themselves. John Baptist's remark reads well in the third chapter of his namesake's Gospel. The text uses a pair of present infinitives, and that tense in Greek contains the notion of a process, a continuity. He said: 'He must go on increasing, and I must go on decreasing'. Let it be added that there is no implied overwhelming and blotting out of the subject in this blessed process. In becoming more and more like Christ a Christian discovers the only way to become, more and more his true self, the person God had from the beginning in mind and purpose. Yes, indeed, that must be every preacher's theme. Mounting the steps of the barrel-like pulpit in the fine old church in Portland Place, my eyes confronted a text pinned under the desk: 'Sir, we would see Jesus'. We must forget about 'bright services'. The subject is enthralling enough and Christianity, life itself, is a deadly serious business. The proclamation, like the Lord's Prayer, which means increasingly more to me, rakes the soul. Worship calls for adoration, but it is in the stillness of the soul, as Elijah was taught, that God speaks.

And as Christ has grown in my experience, so too has the Word. It speaks with ever greater clarity. I have, as I said, in a small red leather volume, passages of poetry which have moved me and I find lines spring to my mind. Newly born Saul Kane in Masefield, for example: 'Jesus drive the coulter deep, and plow my living man from sleep'. Or in life's storms Housman watching the Severn gale toss the Wrekin: 'The wind it plies the saplings double, it blows so hard 'twill soon be done.' Or Browning: 'I was ever a fighter – so – one fight more.' Tennyson, too, in a hundred lines . . .

I am glad the New Testament pictures life as a battle.

We often, unless we slip off to the rear, feel the press of 'foemen leaning on our shield, and roaring on us as we reel.' There are times when we feel like the Anzacs clinging to the cliffs under Sari Bair, and one morning, as day dawned, seeing the sea empty, the big booming ships gone. That cry from the Cross, that agony in the Garden was no play acting. Tempted 'in all points like as we are' he meant those words.

Sceptical Renan whom I quoted, who so paradoxically admired Christ, and yet rejected what he said about himself, remarked strikingly of Christ's words: 'A species of glitter, at once mild and terrible, a divine force, underlines these words, detaches them from the context, and renders them easily distinguishable . . . we feel them vibrate. They translate themselves spontaneously and fit into the narrative naturally . . .' Try the words on the collection of sayings called the Gospel of Thomas found in 1956. Some 'glitter', some are wordy and flat. Thus some could be authentic and how easy are they to pick.

Let me paraphrase that verse about it in the letter to the Hebrews: 'The word of God is alive and potent, beyond any sword that cuts both ways, slicing deep to the place where mind and emotions meet, to that which holds the personality together and feeds it, and tells us what the truth is about our deepest passions and thoughts'. In a phrase, it is the word 'which understands us.'

How often a word of Christ cuts thus, parts the air above us, and shows us what we are. 'The evil man speaks out of the evil he has stored up in his personality.' 'Go and sin no more'. 'Nevertheless not my will . . .' 'Abide in me . . .' And not only the words of the Lord himself, but the whole of the Bible. It is a fortunate man (or is it rather an insensitive man?) who has never known the need to murmur words of Psalm 51 or the last five verses of Romans 8 about himself? I am glad Elijah, Mark, Peter show me that no failure is final. I am comforted to find the gentleness of Christ in Isaiah: 'a bruised reed he will not break, a smoking wick he will not snuff out'. I am glad that his own Prayer is so complete a rosary, leaving no area of life or worship untouched, and that Paul's chapter on love touches all my conduct, and his last verse of the earlier passage, Chapter Eight, solves at a stroke a dozen problems of social life. I am glad he is 'just' as well as 'faithful' to forgive us our sins. And truly I could so continue for this is the book which shows me to myself.

Shall we, as we draw near the end of what may usefully be said, linger a while over some dominant and embracing convictions which flow directly from a Bible-based faith into the processes of life and thought. Those who try to derive a religion from philosophy end in manifold confusion, but from religion a philosophy necessarily derives, if by way of that overworked term we mean a way of looking at life, a 'world-view' as German has it.

Paul has a phrase: 'the power of his resurrection', and those words are sometimes taken to mean a mighty injection of inexplicable force such as that which, they claim, burned the image on the Shroud of Turin at the moment of Christ's rising. Of that mysterious length of linen I shall not speak. It could be genuine, the actual shroud of Jesus, and how it was marked is beyond my explanation. It do not, however, for a moment believe that Paul had any such meaning in mind. The plain and obvious significance of his words is surely: 'the strength which comes from knowing that Christ is alive' – no more.

That was the power which launched a handful of defeated and broken men victoriously upon the world, and that should be the power which animates our daily living. Writing as an historian, I have had much to say about the resurrection of the Lord. I am convinced by the evidence, but a mere intellectual conviction that his appearance after death, and that strange withdrawal which we call the ascension, is truth which the mind can lean upon, is not enough. Like those brought to a new life and vigour by the knowledge, so must we translate conviction into the patterns of our living and the manner of our thought.

I have told in my translation of Brother Lawrence's *Practice of the Presence of God*, how I searched London and Paris as a young man for the French text of that little book of

1693, whose message had gripped me. It chimed with a part of John's Gospel on which, as I have told here, I was so busily engaged. Chapter 15 reached most firmly from the text and laid hold of me, those words spoken, perhaps, in the late Paschal moonlight under the sculptured vine which circled the gate of the temple: 'Abide in me'. I was in a venerable tradition, for the phrase 'in Christ' haunted the early Christians. It recurs again and again in the graffiti of the Catacombs of Rome. It means living in his living presence, one who watches, loves, knows. There lies the Christian's last full outreach of faith, and again I find myself in tune with Emile Caillet who discovered the French Carmelite too. With the material world besieging us and pressing in on our life from every side, it is tempting at times so to feel a part of its enveloping structure, that one who lived two millennia ago recedes, and merges rather with a vanished past than with a living present.

But all life's strength derives from that realisation. It is in the light of it that Scripture speaks. Paul's behest 'pray without ceasing' is comprehended in it, for what Paul meant was not unending liturgy but an unbroken communion, the 'practice of a Presence' with or without words. The firmness with which heart and mind lay hold of such truth is the measure of our peace and the range of our endeavour. It is a lifelong avocation, and it is not for nothing that the images which the New Testament invokes to describe Christian living are so often metaphors of strife, and a goal or a victory to be attained. Paul writing to his friends in Philippi, in the same context as that in which he pictured life as a chariot-race with the committed charioteer 'reaching out' to clutch the reins over the horses' back, said: 'It is not as though I have reached what I want to reach, or were already perfect, but I press on to lay hold of it – that for which Christ has laid hold of me.'

What else, as I muse thus on the active and enabling thoughts which flow from the faith I hold? This – the operation of God's wisdom. It is an elusive conviction, demanding patience and at times stretching faith to breaking point. But if God is love and is also wise, is there not the guarantee that those committed to his care can be certain that, as Phillips renders Romans 8:28, 'all things fit into a pattern for good'? I have written boldly at length on this in a little book of full two years ago in which I told why, after a lifetime, I am still a Christian. I say 'boldly' because it is the area of life which is likely to be subjected to the severest testings, and it is the way with man that, however often understanding comes with the years, the harsher trials of life can still stir consternation.

Mine is not a Lord who strews my path with roses, finds me a parking place and strikes down the foe before our swords have crossed, but he had turned, over wide tracts of experience, what I thought disaster into triumph, lifted me from stumbling, pressed hard on all unworthiness, blessings beyond all listing, and a satisfying purpose in life. If the way is hard as I reach the last ridges, can I not go on believing that he who has led will lead on?

I cannot tell how much longer the way is to the fords of Jordan, but, long or short, the Bible and I will always go together now. It tells me, however desolate and lonely the path, really I am not alone. It leaves agonising questions unsolved, but assures me that none are not included in the wise plan which embraces all of life.

I quoted Peter: 'Lord, to whom shall we go? You tell us about a different kind of life altogether'. 'There is no other stream', as Aslan said to Jill when she feared to pass him to reach the water. With that, I think, I have no more to say, and it is at that point that those who think words are too precious to waste, cease their speaking or writing.